MW00334799

the OTH
JOURNA

the OTHER JOURNAL

THE FOOD AND FLOURISHING ISSUE

Copyright © 2012 *The Other Journal*. All rights reserved. Except for brief quotations in critical publications or reviews, no part of this book may be reproduced in any manner without prior written permission from the publisher. Write: Permissions, Wipf and Stock Publishers, 199 W. 8th Ave., Suite 3, Eugene, OR 97401.

Cascade Books
An Imprint of Wipf and Stock Publishers
199 W. 8th Ave., Suite 3
Eugene, OR 97401
www.wipfandstock.com

ISSN: 1933-7957
ISBN: 13: 978-1-60899-968-2

Scripture quotations marked ESV are from The Holy Bible, English Standard Version®, copyright © 2001 by Crossway, a publishing ministry of Good News Publishers. Used by permission. All rights reserved.

Scripture quotations marked (KJV) are taken from the King James Version.

Scripture quotations marked NAB are taken from the *New American Bible, revised edition, copyright* © 2010, 1991, 1986, 1970 by the Confraternity of Christian Doctrine, Washington, DC, and are used by permission of the copyright owner. All Rights Reserved. No part of the New American Bible may be reproduced in any form without permission in writing from the copyright owner.

Scripture quotations marked NIV are taken from the Holy Bible, New International Version®, NIV®, copyright © 1973, 1978, 1984, 2011 by Biblica, Inc.™ Used by permission of Zondervan. All rights reserved worldwide.

Scripture quotations marked RSV are taken from the Revised Standard Version of the Bible, copyright © 1952 [2nd edition, 1971] by the Division of Christian Education of the National Council of the Churches of Christ in the United States of America. Used by permission. All rights reserved.

Scripture quotations marked NRSV are taken from the New Revised Standard Version Bible, copyright © 1989 by the Division of Christian Education of the National Council of the Churches of Christ in the United States of America. Used by permission. All rights reserved.

On the cover: Lee Price, *Sleeping with Peaches*, 2011, oil on linen, 56 x 81 in. Courtesy of private collector.

Manufactured in the U.S.A.

The Other Journal is based at the Seattle School of Theology and Psychology

THE OTHER JOURNAL

Chris Keller :: Editor-in-Chief, Co-Founder
Andrew David :: Managing Editor
Tom Ryan :: Executive Editor
Jon Stanley :: Theology Editor
Allison Backous: Creative Writing Editor
John Totten :: Music and Film Reviews Editor
Heather Smith Stringer :: Art Editor
Ben Suriano :: Assistant Theology Editor

Dan Rhodes :: Assistant Theology Editor
Seth Rash :: Assistant Editor
Ian Knippel :: Executive Producer of Video Content
Eric Borgh :: Intern
Molly Farrell :: Intern
Caitlin Watkins :: Intern
Nathaniel T. Rogers :: Intern

EDITORIAL ADVISORY BOARD

Brian Bantum
Daniel Bell Jr.
Jason Byassee
William T. Cavanaugh
Pam Cochran
David Dark
Dwight Friesen
Amy Laura Hall

Peter Heltzel
Paula Huston
Fr. Emmanuel Katongole
Jeffrey Keuss
Ron Kuipers
D. Stephen Long
Charles Marsh
Charles Mathewes

Eugene McCarraher
Brian McLaren
Alison Milbank
John Milbank
Debra Rienstra
Luci Shaw
James K. A. Smith
Graham Ward

SUBSCRIPTIONS

The Other Journal (ISSN: 1933-7957) is published twice a year at the annual rates listed below.

USA Individuals: 1 year $25.00
USA Institutions: 1 year $50.00
Canadian Individuals & Institutions: 1 year USA rate + $4.00 shipping
International Individuals & Institutions: 1 year USA rate + $15.00 shipping

CONTACT INFORMATION

Send all article submissions and queries to submissions@theotherjournal.com

Or mail to:
The Other Journal
2501 Elliott Avenue
Seattle, WA 98121

Subscriptions may be placed online at www.theotherjournal.com/subscriptions

Subscription e-mail: subscriptions@theotherjournal.com
Advertising e-mail: advertising@theotherjournal.com
Phone: 206-876-6100
Website: www.theotherjournal.com

Contents

Letter from the Editors

WHEN WE COME TO the Communion table, we participate in the literal and symbolic culmination of our worship and our lives as Christians. It is an occasion of remembrance and reflection and mystery that both brings us a foretaste of our future communion with God and brings us together as a people. It was at this table where both royalty and peasants received nourishment, an act that, if only in symbol, united them as equals. And it is here that people of differing histories, cultures, and classes can still celebrate together as often as we remember him.

The centrality of food to our worship speaks to its power to shape our lives. The sights and smells of food become the thing of memory, they become the taste of childhood or love or grief, and yet they also propel us forward to future faithfulness. As we gather, prepare, and consume food, we unite our daily routines and needs with the earth and its creatures, transforming God's bounty into sustenance, pleasure, and community.

And yet our culture sends us mixed messages about food that diminish our sense of these connections. In the dizzying array of grocery food products, fast food restaurants, and twenty-four-hour cooking shows, we learn to take the gift, grace, and community of a good meal for granted. We become alienated from our food's source and forgetful of its meaning. Or as Stephen H. Webb notes in his essay "Against the Gourmands," we become one with a culture where gluttony is glamorous and hip, where we build Babel-like towers of textured vegetable protein and soy products to the glory of our eco-friendly taste buds. Food can become our everything. And it can become our enemy—waging a war of obesity against our bodies, pushing us to greater and greater lengths to lose those extra pounds.

Issue #19 of *The Other Journal* examines these complex relationships between our selves, our culture, and our food from a theological bent. The thoughtful contributors to this issue—William T. Cavanaugh, Matthew Dickerson, David Grumett, John Leax, Alissa Wilkinson, Norman Wirzba, and many others—take us to Middle-earth and the Romanian city of Constanța. They swing by swank Manhattan bistros and raucous NFL stadiums on game day. But most importantly, they return us to the Communion table and to that first garden where God walked with us and gave us the gift of his creation.

—*The Other Journal* editorial team

1 The Catch

by R O B E R T   H I L L   L O N G

The fish she bears in the basket on her head
lost their gleam between boat and market, lost it
the moment they had nothing to breathe but air.
Stunned pewter, they sway toward a mound of ice
built for them—a mausoleum that will vanish
at the end of day, when their migratory journey
resumes within bodies that swim in sweaty beds
toward a stillness called sleep. But for now

they fend off the sun's daily query—
Are you hungry?—to the woman who mounts
a stairway of cobble where each step is lit
by sunrise. She keeps balance. Her imagining
does not extend to airplanes or electricity.
She does not believe all that dies dies blind.

2 Against the Gourmands:
In Praise of Fast Food as a Form of Fasting

by STEPHEN H. WEBB

F OOD IS FUEL MUCH the same way that wood is fuel. The fact that you can build a house with wood alters its combustible properties no more than the fact that you can create a banquet with food alters its digestible properties. Even in the form of a house, wood remains fuel, which is why houses can burn down, just as food remains fuel even in the form of fancy hors d'oeuvres and haute cuisine, which is why eating too much can make your gut burn up. Food is a form of energy, and our relationship to it is essentially one of exchange so that the most basic rule of eating is that we need to spend less energy in acquiring food than it yields in consuming it. Everything else is, well, sauces and gravies.

Food is also, of course, an expression of cultural values and a reflection of so-cial organization. We are no more content to reduce a meal to its caloric essentials than we are happy to live in a wood shack. We want our meals and our shelters to say something about who we are and what we believe. That is why both dinners and houses can strive to be works of art, even though they do not have to be anything more than plants and sticks. We eat to stay alive, and we eat to make something more of our lives than merely staying alive, but nature can be remarkably stingy, which makes cooking, for many people, more of a necessity than an art. Indeed, for most of human history, and even today in most parts of the world, the majority of people do not have the luxury to treat either food or wood as more than fuel.

I begin this essay with these basic observations because I think, in an era when many of the cultural elite want to promote more healthy eating in the form of more simple living, it is important to remind ourselves that today's trendy diets do not necessarily get us back to a more natural diet, whatever that might be. Only when nature is bountiful can we cultivate reasons for why and what we eat, which means that, paradoxically, we can begin to imagine what a natural diet might be only when we live at some significant distance from the vagaries of nature. The oven timer cannot be turned back to some more primitive, simpler time: the more natural the diet, the more it will need to be artfully (that is, artificially) produced. It should be no surprise, then, that at the very moment when processed foods are at their most pervasive, the most important rationale governing our diet is the mandate to eat more naturally, even though, in even the simplest diet, it is hard to distinguish the natural from the fanciful. After all, Americans are crafty consumers who want to maximize all of their many self-interests. To sell smart eating, food producers must please the palate, healthify the heart, and cater to the conscience. Banquets of the pagan variety (think ancient Rome) are out (even though all-you-can-eat buffets still cater to the lower classes), but they have been replaced with gourmet meals with a countercultural agenda. Americans want their smaller, hormone-free portions to be morally as well as physically satisfying. Food must be as good for the soul as the stomach.

As a supporter of free markets and an optimist (for the most part) about technology, I think these culinary trends are basically good. American consumerism keeps corporations on their toes, forcing markets to adapt to cultural changes. Indeed, at the risk of seeming disengaged and complacent, I don't spend much time worrying about changing dietary practices. If human nature is uniform and constant, as I believe it to be, then bad dietary choices have a natural limit, and we have probably reached that limit in our snack-obsessed culture. Humans can only do so much damage to themselves without a self-corrective movement becoming inevitable. Species commit collective suicide only in science fiction movies and politicized apocalyptic scenarios.

What I do worry about, however, is some of the rhetoric behind dietary trends. In the ancient world, diet was a matter of religious custom and metaphysical belief, but the case can be made that Christianity secularized the production and consumption of food by taking the ritual out of animal sacrifices. Eating for Christians could still be ceremonial, but what you ate and how you prepared it was of no ultimate concern. How else could the Apostle Paul have traveled the world depending on the hospitality of strangers? Christianity preached a universal message that rendered dietary differences trivial by making them a matter of personal or familial choice. Today, however, with our modern hunger for more connection to the natural world, diet has once again become a matter of grave spiritual concern. Given the tendency of our culture to treat religion as a matter of free-floating spiritual power, always ready to attach itself to a new host, it was only a matter of time until modern people started saying such things as "you are what you eat." Without any traditions that bind us to the past, we are left to pick and choose how we want food to reflect our values and beliefs. When Christianity is thrown into the mix, a cafeteria of theological options is the result. Christian beliefs can end up validating and promoting dietary practices that might have more to do with fantasies about opting out of modernity than the reality of following Jesus Christ.

Food is powerful because hunger is powerful, and of all bodily pleasures, eating provides the most constant and variable occasion of physical satisfaction. For that reason, the morality of eating is always positioned between calls for self-discipline that can end up silencing bodily desires and invitations to social celebrations that can turn into excuses for gluttony. Given this limited grammar of moral meaning, we should not be too gullible about the potential of elevating the gustatory to grand moral meaning making. The attempt to return to more natural eating, whether in the form of buying local produce or immersing oneself in the arcane knowledge of how best to grill root vegetables, does not constitute a protest against the modern world and its capitalist masters any more than being able to discuss the much contested aromatic effects of arugula is a sign of advanced spiritual awareness and heightened cultural sensitivity. We face in food the same range of moral considerations as the ancients, and they understood that the basic dilemma of eating concerns the problem not so much of overeating (since you can only eat so much) but of overvaluing eating. We naturally want to enhance the basic biological function of food by refining its flavors in order to heighten its effects. We want food to touch every part of us. It is as if we want to make love to what we eat.

Today, such refinements take the idealized form of sifting through ingredients in order to weigh the morality of their origins as well as their consequences, but I do not think this changes the basic situation of humanity and food. Indeed, throughout the whole of Christian history, with the exception of the most recent past, no theologian would have made a distinction between the gluttony of the ravenous and ill-mannered who, given an opportunity to eat like kings and queens, act like animals, and the gluttony of the upper classes who, given the resources to afford to fidget and fuss with their food, build towers of Babel made of meat and pastries (or, today, soy products and textured vegetable protein). Gluttony is gluttony, even if it is in the service of celebrating social events.

Whether it is in the form of sumptuous vegetarian delights that go down easier than the moral message they artfully conceal or carefully grilled free-range meat that speaks, through its intimate surroundings of spare vegetables and the latest discovery of a primitive whole grain, of the quiet pleasures of reserve and restraint, the good meal today is a mixed bag of kitchen craftsmanship, a painfully discriminating objectivity regarding flavor, and an insider's knowledge of how far one must travel to find the best combination of local produce and local color (that is, a good story about a farmer kicking the corporate habit). Foodies have turned the dining room into a classroom and chewing into a means of sparking serious synaptic brain activity. Far from being an exercise in authenticity, gourmet dining, even when it is conducted in a stately puritan spirit, is an aesthetic performance, and in fact, no matter how artfully enacted, it is never more than a minor genre in the category of staged productions. Food, that is, remains a means to two ends, one biological and the other social.

For these reasons, I propose that fast food reveals the essence of nourishment better than the latest recipes from *Gourmet* or *Bon Appetit* magazines. However, "fast food" is such a gut-wrenchingly pejorative phrase that any discussion of it requires an objective definition. Fast food, for the purposes of this essay, is food that is produced and consumed efficiently. It is, in a word, fuel. Others might define fast food as food that is unhealthy, but there is no reason why food that is prepared and eaten quickly must be bad for you. On the contrary, as I will argue later on, fast food is becoming healthier all the time, and there is no reason to think that it will not continue to develop in that direction.

If I am right about fast food representing food as fuel, then what about food as an expression of cultural values and a reflection of social organization? For Christians, the answer to that question should be obvious. Even in the Eucharist food is fuel, but this is the one meal that shows us what food can and should be when it is treated as more than just fuel. The Eucharist is a simple meal that presents the reality of Jesus Christ, upon whose presence our souls best feast when our own bodies fast. I use the word *fast* in that sentence due not only to the longstanding practice in the Christian tradition of fasting before receiving the Eucharist but also due to the nature of the meal itself. Although it is easy to overlook the fact that the Eucharist is a meal, I want to argue that its material elements are not just token items that carry merely symbolic value. The centrality of the plate and cup are perhaps best indicated by how hard it is to imagine the Eucharist as anything other than bread and wine (or grape juice). If the Eucharist were purely symbolic, then the Lord's Supper could be replaced with other food items (say, milk and chocolate, which indeed was the case at a Unitarian Church I once visited) or even other means altogether (say, inner prayer or a Eucharist of the heart, as with the Quakers). This meal has a predetermined (and limited!) menu not only because Jesus Christ commanded it but also because no other act matches eating's intimacy and no other foods correlate so fittingly with what this ritual enacts. This meal gives us the full (and, for Roman Catholics, the bodily) presence of Jesus, flesh and blood, and in consuming this meal we become one with him. By opening up (indeed, literally opening our insides) to the real, physical presence of Jesus, we become one with him.

The Eucharist shows us what food can be when it is not just fuel precisely because, in this meal, food itself becomes something different from what it ordinarily is. Throughout human history, of course, food has always been more than just fuel, but for Christians, this something *more* has to be nothing less than what happens in Holy Communion. Just as Jesus Christ is the firstborn of creation (Col 15), the bread and wine, after they have been consecrated, are the firstfruits of the new creation that is witnessed to by the whole Bible. All of nature is groaning for redemption (Rom 8:18–23), and the world to come will still be recognizable as a real world, with glorified matter to sustain our glorified bodies. In the Eucharist, we receive a foretaste of this transformation. We taste the bread and wine, but we are filled with the Holy Spirit, and the pleasure of consumption lifts our hearts up to God. We have a sense, no matter how partial or incomplete, of a new food, manna from heaven that, once eaten, preserves us from death (John 6:51).

When food is more than fuel, then, it is a gift of the Father comprised of the Son and energized by the Holy Spirit. This meal is the paradigm of all meals, and as such, it should not be corrupted by differences of taste or culinary skill. Some early Christians did want to turn this meal into a feast, but the Apostle Paul insisted that it remain what it is—a simple meal with an overabundance of grace and glory (1 Cor 11:17–34). Paul understood that its simplicity guaranteed the way it could overcome social and cultural divisions among those partaking of it. Paul was especially concerned about those who, when it came time to eat the Lord's Supper, turned their noses up at the common fare of the lowest classes, which, after all, is what bread and (watered) wine is. Nonetheless, by disciplining those who wanted the Eucharist to be more than a simple meal, Paul inadvertently contributed to the idea that it is not a meal at all. "What! Do you not have homes to eat and drink in?" he asked the Corinthians (11:22 ESV). Paul wanted to keep gluttony out of the church (some people were bringing and consuming enough wine to get drunk), but he did not want to keep food out of the Eucharist. On the contrary, he wanted Christians to learn how to eat by attending this meal. Just as children learn their manners from eating with adults, Christians learn what it means to be a member of Christ's body by partaking of God with each other.

So what does this have to do with health food and foodie magazines and local produce? I am certainly not saying that every meal should be limited to bread and wine, although this was an ideal that monastic Christians were known to strive for in the Middle Ages. It also does not mean that every meal should be somber and serious, although there is something to be said for the monastic tradition—a staple of Benedictine practice—of listening to someone read from a good book during meals. In fact, the idea that the Eucharist is a time to reflect only on sin and not also on our liberation from sin (and thus the joy that comes from Christ) is a modern invention that has little evidential support in the Bible or early church history (which is why Paul was always trying to get Christians to be a bit more circumspect at Communion). No, every meal should aim toward the Eucharist in the sense that we should eat with glad hearts expressing gratitude to God, inviting others into our meals as well as treating all food as potential emblems of divine mercy.

There is something to be said, then, for the argument that locally grown produce and humanely raised animal products capture and extend the moral message of Communion. In Christianity, however, these dietary decisions flow naturally from acts of worshipping God, not efforts to change the world. Moreover, Christianity reminds us that only when we bring the fruits of our labor to God can we hope to resist the temptation of making those fruits look better than they really are. When we try to make meals a means of moralistic debate, we demean the gifted character of nature's provisions. When we try to inject morality into our meals, we inevitably take too much pleasure from our actions and mistake physical satisfaction for a sense of social accomplishment.

The Eucharist is not merely symbolic, but we can turn all of our meals into symbols of it, and only by doing so can we hope to make good eating an instance of doing good. The problem is that the bread and wine in the Eucharist become sacraments when they are consecrated. They are not sacraments before that act, and we thus cheapen the Eucharist when we think of food itself as sacramental. Much of the foodie critique of fast food is based on this mistaken notion that the longer it takes to make and consume a meal, the more spiritual it is. Devoting oneself to the kitchen is not a devotional act in the strictly theological sense. Food is a drug (just ask the US Food and Drug Administration), which should tell us that fine dining is to the tongue and nose what a sexual orgy is to other bodily organs. In both cases, sensations have to be carefully paced and systematically parsed if satiation is to be postponed. In any case, the proliferation of televised cooking shows demonstrates that the pleasures of taste have penetrated the eyes almost as much as the pleasures of sex.

Frozen pizzas, canned vegetables, cheap hamburgers, and sugary beverages are not the enemy; we are, which suggests that junk food is not the real temptation: pride is. When we regulate one desire, we inevitably take pleasure in another. When vegetarians give up meat, they find compensation by granting themselves the right to tell other people what to eat. Liberal academics who rant against Walmart and McDonald's are the moral equivalent of dieters who secretly indulge in french fries: the regimen of most scholars is typically so focused, restrained, and vigilant that the sheer fun of making sweeping generalizations about the lower classes is, on occasion, irresistible. Everyday sinning is not very original, but original sin is very creative. We have a bottomless capacity to derive moral gratification from our sensual sacrifices.

That bad things happen theologically when these points are lost is illustrated by William T. Cavanaugh's cleverly titled book *Being Consumed*. Subtitled *Economics and Christian Desire*, Cavanaugh bemoans the free market for not making moral judgments about the value of each and every economic transaction. The "free market has no *telos*, that is, no common end to which desire is directed."[1] As a result, capitalism consumes our souls because it sells us nothing but the pleasure of wanting what we do not have. "Shopping," he writes, "not buying itself, is the heart of consumerism" (47). Capitalism is not about helping us to earn (and therefore learn) what we want. In fact, capitalism is innovative in the way that it directs greed toward not the accumulation of objects but the liberation of desire. In his words, "The key question in every transaction is whether or not the transaction contributes to the flourishing of each person involved, and this question can only be judged, from a theological point of view, according to the end of life, which is participation in the life of God" (viii). Cavanaugh seems to think that unless an ultimate theological end is the direct aim of every economic act, then those acts have no morally serious meaning. Every purchase we make must be theologically correct.

The most immediate problem with this argument is that it confuses two very different levels of analysis. From the assumption that the free market has no overarching aim he draws the conclusion that every individual acts out of sheer caprice:

> Where there are no objectively desirable ends, and the individual is
> told to choose his or her own ends, then choice itself becomes the

1. William T. Cavanaugh, *Being Consumed: Economics and Christian Desire* (Grand Rapids: Eerdmans, 2008) 5. Further citations to this book will give page numbers parenthetically in the text.

only thing that is inherently good. When there is a recession, we are told to buy things to get the economy going; *what* we buy makes no difference. All desires, good and bad, melt into the one overriding imperative to consume, and we all stand under the one sacred canopy of consumption for its own sake. (13, italics original)

The conclusion, however, is unearned. Even if the market as a whole has no clear moral aim, it is not the case that individuals enter the market with only a generalized desire to buy. Cavanaugh seems to think that the economy and consumption are related by a vicious circle, in that they exist for each other and nothing else, but people participate in the market in order to achieve their personal goals, which include commitments to family, religion, and charity toward others.

Desire is always objective; it is always desire *for*, even if it is desire for an object only because that object is the means of a certain kind of experience. It is true that Americans are sometimes encouraged to spend in order to help bolster the economy, but it does not follow that they squander their money for no specific purpose. Even if someone were to be forced (by an "overriding imperative") to consume, in a free market they would still have the freedom to choose what particular product they want to consume. This would involve prioritizing their desires according to some scale of value.

But even Cavanaugh's initial assumption—that the free market has no overarching goal or aim—needs to be questioned. The fact that individuals are free to use their own values to order their purchasing practices does not mean that the economy as a whole has no goal or end. Economic growth is necessary for the survival and flourishing of human society; economic depressions, by not creating jobs, cause both social and individual instability. Cavanaugh himself is ambiguous about his own declaration that capitalism is amoral or at least morally vacuous, given that he actually thinks the free market necessarily entails a strong moral assumption about freedom, even though he puts that assumption in the most negative light. Cavanaugh thinks that capitalism defines freedom negatively as freedom from interference, but capitalism defines freedom in this way only in reference to economic exchange. Negative freedom is not a global definition but a very specific definition of what freedom looks like under the conditions of a competitive market, and even in the market, negative freedom is not an accurate description of freedom, given that most free market advocates accept the need for various kinds of (minimal) regulation.

The shortcomings of Cavanaugh's analysis are most obvious when he talks about food. "Before I read Michael Pollan," he writes, "I had only the vaguest sense of how beef is typically raised" (31). Pollan is a popular writer who, far from being a vegetarian, has written in *New York Times Magazine* about his adventures in buying a steer, shooting a wild pig, and throwing a thirty-six-hour dinner party that included a whole roasted goat (October 10, 2010). Pollan is, in a word, a gourmand, which is the same word in French for a glutton. Interestingly, although there are many theologians who write about the ethics of diet, religion is a topic that Pollan studiously avoids. Cavanaugh tells the story of how, after reading Pollan, he began buying his meat from the Zweber family farm, where the cows are grass fed and hormone-free. "When I buy beef from them," he claims, "it is a truly free exchange" (31). What makes it free, evidently, is neither the animals (he does not tell us how they are slaughtered) nor the price (you pay for the high quality) but the nature of the exchange: "All the information I need is available and transparent. . . . My exchange with the supermarket is less than free, because the information I need is not readily available to me" (31). Information, in fact, is exactly what Cavanaugh is buying from the Zwebers, because they tell him exactly what he wants to know about the health of the animals he will eat, the ecological balance of the land they occupy, and the purity of the resources they consume. What the Zwebers do not publicize, of course, is the hidden costs of raising meat for both the environment and human well-being.

Cavanaugh's story of the Zweber family farm is meant to illustrate the value of buying locally as a check on the menace of multinational corporations, the hyper-mobility of capital, and the false universality of globalization. I am not saying that there is anything wrong with buying locally, but Cavanaugh fails to recognize just how capitalistic the Zwebers of the world are. Hormone-free farmers are responding to consumers, and once a niche market becomes popular with the masses, it must match growth with increasing efficiency. In other words, if everyone wanted to drive out into the country for free-range meat, demand would outstrip supply, the price would go up, and somebody would figure out a way to lower prices by linking, organizing, and expanding the various production sites. Free range would go corporate (and this, of course, is already happening). Cavanaugh holds up the local as the choice everyone should make, but if everyone were to make that choice, it could no longer be local.

The corporatization of health food would be a bad thing in Cavanaugh's book, but not in mine. Getting better food to the greatest number of people is what capitalism is all about. The irony, of course, is that Cavanaugh describes himself as a consumer, and he is a good one at that—creating demand for new kinds of products that will be useful for everyone. Consumption is passive only in the handbooks of leftists, who always tend to portray the masses as victims of somebody else's power. Buying new products—as many of us know from the box of useless electronic gadgets we have sitting in a closet—is risky business. Economists call the practice "early adoption," and Americans get excited about new products faster than anyone else. Active consumers like Cavanaugh encourage investors to invest and inventors to invent. Early adopters also provide crucial feedback for the improvement of products. Consumers, in other words, have kept the American economy growing and have pushed American business to the front of the pack.

I have no doubt that consumers like Cavanaugh and countless others will continue to pressure food corporations to make better products. A recent *New Yorker* article on PepsiCo, the monster of the munchies, does a good job of documenting this trend (John Seabrook, May 16, 2011). The largest snack food company in the United States is preparing for future growth by developing drinkable oatmeal, new salt and sugar substitutes, and chilled gazpacho to go with an edible spoon. I have no doubt too that in vitro meat (sci-fi sausage, petri pork, beaker bacon—call it what you want) will, once it is developed enough to be marketable, wipe out many of the environmental and health disadvantages of factory-farmed meat. Once food prices become too high, consumers will turn to cultured meat for its lower price, with savings in water and grain consumption being the icing on the cake. I am not saying that I will rush to buy it; I try to minimize my meat intake, and cultured meat, to me, will simply reveal what meat essentially is: industrialized decaying muscle matter that is seasoned to appeal to the lowest of human tastes. Once in vitro meat takes over the market, there will probably still be a few Zweber farms left, catering to the anticorporate crowd and the naturalist zealots. But the planet will be cleaner, fewer animals will be kept in inhumane conditions, and global hunger will be much diminished.

Consumers are driving the health food market because people desire not just what is available. They also desire what they wish they could have. Desire is forward-looking; we want the future to be different from the past. In theological terms, desire is essentially eschatological in its anticipation of a better world that is always not yet available to us. Even corporations desire a better future, given that, if they are in business for the long haul, it is in their own best interests. Evidence for this assertion can be found in the story of Walmart, which has become a leader in the merging of sustainable and profitable business practices.[2] I am not denying that desire is also, no matter how forward-looking, always mired in self-centered motivations, but it is important to distinguish between a critique of desire and a cynical attitude toward how other people spend their money. All that the term *consumerism* adds to the more traditional tropes of greed and gluttony is the perverse notion that capitalism, precisely because it is so successful in raising standards of living for so many people, provides a wider range of occasions for sin, as if *Playboy* magazine invented lust. There is no psychological law that says that the poor are less greedy than those who have a higher standard of living. Greed is relative, as is wealth itself. Only a moralist with a pedigree in socialist nostalgia and a casuistical calculator in his pocket could think that capitalism lies at the origin of original sin.

I should point out that Cavanaugh insists that he is not advocating for socialism, a form of government that was, nonetheless, inspired by the goal that he shares of having morality micromanage the market. Interestingly enough, he rejects socialism because it would make markets more inefficient—"I believe it would be counterproductive to expect the state to attempt to impose such a direction on economic activities. What is most important is the direct embodiment of free economic practices" (32). The church should be in control of the market, not the government. Far from proposing a sectarian withdrawal from a world corrupted by capitalism, Cavanaugh wants the church to become a haven for fair trading. Personally, I am more hopeful of minimal, cost-effective government regulation of the market than I am of the church effecting global change by having "farmers sell their produce directly through local congregations" (87). I kind of like the idea of church potlucks becoming a celebration of local produce, but doesn't this risk introducing the very class divisions that the Apostle Paul, when he advised Christians to eat at home, feared? Won't those who bring garden veggies to the table look down on those who make a green bean casserole from the can?

Cavanaugh bases the dubious idea of ecclesial countercapitalism on the Eucharist. Indeed, Cavanaugh is well known for drawing political lessons from church ritual.[3] The Eucharist slows down time and opens up space for a reconfiguration of our relationship to God and others, and thus it should have an impact on everything we do, without exception, but I have a hard time seeing it as a paradigm of the slow

2. See Edward Humes, *Force of Nature: The Unlikely Story of Wal-Mart's Green Revolution* (New York: HarperBusiness, 2011).

3. See William T. Cavanaugh, *Torture and Eucharist: Theology, Politics, and the Body of Christ*, Challenges in Contemporary Theology (Malden, MA: Blackwell, 1998).

food movement. For Cavanaugh, the Eucharist resists the culture of consumption because "the consumer of the Eucharist is taken up into a larger body, the body of Christ" (54). Cavanaugh's idea of the Eucharist is of Christ consuming us, not us consuming Christ. The Eucharist thus erases all individual boundaries and social borders: "The very distinction between what is mine and what is yours breaks down in the body of Christ" (56). We are left with the rather grotesque image of our bodies becoming food for Christ, rather than Christ putting an end to sacrifice by giving himself to us. Cavanaugh needs this image because he wants to claim that becoming a member of Christ's body overturns the right of private property, but history has taught us many tragic times that private property can only be banished by a very large government. Cavanaugh's rhetoric is potent because it smacks of a longing for the kind of unity that, in the twentieth century, was the promise (and peril) of socialism. The idea that distinctions between me and you break down in the body of Christ is not even biblical, given that Paul makes a point of saying that this body is composed of parts with different functions (Rom 12:4).

Far from being a ritual that creates an organic unity so compressed that it defies individuality, the Eucharist asks each partaker to become Christlike, and that transformation begins, significantly, with the consumption of a simple meal. We are to become holy through, among other virtues, frugality, not collective ownership of private property. And that returns us to the topic of fast food. Fast food for many Americans is valuable precisely because it is frugal—in terms of saving time if not ecological resources. When I eat fast food it is almost always because I do not care that much about what I am eating, precisely because there is something I need to get to that I really care about (and it usually has to do with a family event). Fast food as a kind of fasting is essentially an acknowledgement that food is a means and not an end in itself. Even the food of the Eucharist is a means, because the body of Christ is what we are really consuming—and far from being consumed by Christ's body we are made holy by Christ in order to give ourselves to others. Yes, family time should be protected by preserving the rituals of the family meal, but there is nothing particularly Christian about the dinner hour, no matter how sacred most of us think it is. There is only one meal we should not miss, and there is only one meal that is perfect in every way, so much so that you leave not wanting anything more, and that is the meal that gives us a foretaste of the kingdom yet to come. In comparison, every other meal is just fuel, no matter how good it tastes.

3 Out to Lunch: A Response to Stephen Webb's "Against the Gourmands"

by WILLIAM T. CAVANAUGH

THE FILM *BABETTE'S FEAST* has perhaps done more service in teaching undergraduates and seminarians about the Eucharist than any other work of art over the last twenty-five years. It is the tale of an austere Danish Christian sect that carefully shuns the sensual delights of this world. Babette, a star chef and a refugee from counterrevolutionary violence in Paris, comes to live among the dwindling congregation. After winning 10,000 francs in the French lottery, Babette decides to spend it all on a sumptuous banquet on the occasion of the hundredth anniversary of the founder's birth. The congregation, afraid of the sin of sensual luxury, decides to eat the meal but not to take any pleasure in it and to avoid all mention of the food during the dinner. They cannot help but be overcome by the meal, however, and gradually their frigid facades melt, while old hostilities are repaired and old loves rekindled. The film is a mainstay in the classroom because of its deliberate Eucharistic imagery. Babette's total gift is a symbol of Christ's self-emptying and Christ's call to the table of abundance. The congregation gradually accepts, despite their resistance, that God's grace is not finite but lavishly spread over all of creation. They are invited to a meal that, in its celebration of God's creation and redemption, offers a glimpse of a new world in which sins are forgiven and all that divides us is healed.

As I read Stephen Webb's essay "Against the Gourmands," I could not help but picture the members of the Danish congregation, shutting their eyes and trying desperately not to take pleasure in the feast laid out before them.[1] Webb denies that food

1. All quotations from Webb are taken from the previous article, Webb, "Against the Gourmands: In Praise of Fast Food as a Form of Fasting," 2–13.

is sacramental and subscribes to a kind of dualism in which, as he says, "fine dining is to the tongue and nose what a sexual orgy is to other bodily organs. In both cases, sensations have to be carefully paced and systematically parsed if satiation is to be postponed." We can agree that overindulgence of the senses is certainly problematic, but I don't have the same qualms about a sacramental view of food or the world in general. In principle, at least, it is entirely scriptural to see all creation as an icon of God and a potential window to God's grace. Gluttony is a sin; Webb is surely right to say that Christians should not elevate the self-indulgent aesthetic appreciation of fine cuisine into a virtue. Just as surely, however, there is a distinction to be made between a properly sacramental point of view and an idolatrous one that simply collapses the divine into the material.

It would be fair enough if Webb's essay were simply a reminder that refining our tastes will not save our souls. Where Webb's essay really goes wrong, however, is in its refusal to make another type of distinction: that between the gourmand and the ordinary people who are trying to return some measure of justice and sanity to a corporatized food system which has become exploitative of farmers and workers and toxic to the environment. Webb lumps together snobs who consider knowledge of the "aromatic effects of arugula" to be a sign of advanced spiritual awareness with people who guarantee a fair wage for local farmers by forming community supported agriculture (CSA) cooperative buying arrangements. In this manner, Webb manages to present the local food movement—arguably one of most successful grassroots, democratic forms of resistance to concentrated power in the United States in the last few decades—as a form of elitism. To this irony is added the fact that Webb sets himself against the elite while rushing to the defense of corporate agriculture and behemoths like Walmart and McDonald's.

Webb is rightly concerned that those who shop at Walmart not be considered less Christian than or morally inferior to those who can afford to shop at Whole Foods. But to move from here to a blanket approval for the "efficiency" of the current food system requires ignoring the fact that the reason many are forced by necessity to take advantage of Walmart's low, low prices is that low, low prices come at the expense of low, low wages. Walmart in particular has been ruthless in its demands that suppliers cut costs, which means low wages in the United States and even lower wages in China. Walmart is by no means alone; "efficiency" means low wages and brutal working conditions for immigrants—many undocumented—who work the fields and slaughterhouses of the corporatized food system. Webb dismisses "sifting through ingredients in order to weigh the morality of their origins as well as their consequences" as just another form of high-culture gluttony. Although it is true that not everyone has the resources required to track down and buy food produced in a way that is healthy for human communities, it is not that difficult to distinguish between gluttony on the one hand and a concern for avoiding the exploitation of the poor on the other.

Because of his conflation of mere aestheticism with social justice, Webb continually diverts attention from the social consequences of the current system. For example, he writes that "Much of the foodie critique of fast food is based on this mistaken notion that the longer it takes to make and consume a meal, the more spiritual it is." This may be the "foodie" critique, but it is not the far more serious critique mounted by Eric Schlosser and others. As Schlosser points out, fast food has had a tendency to distort the food system through the pursuit of the very "efficiency" Webb extols.[2] Schlosser's *Fast Food Nation* is not a rant against the tastes of the lower classes but a sobering exploration of the often-ruinous effects of the present system on independent farmers and ranchers, the environment, farm workers, slaughterhouse workers, rural communities, and more. Besides low wages, the current food system provides cheap "fuel" for us because it externalizes many of the true costs; what we don't pay at the drive-through window, we pay through taxes for government subsidies, higher health-care costs, wars for cheap oil, environmental cleanups, et cetera.

Likewise, simple living and organic food are, at the very least, more than an artificial attempt to foster a certain "natural" aesthetic by the cultural elite. Webb claims that "the more natural the diet, the more it will need to be artfully (that is, artificially) produced," but this is misleading at best. The only reason organic food is considered exotic today is that farming through chemicals gained almost complete hegemony in the second half of the twentieth century, largely through the concerted efforts of chemical companies and the US Department of Agriculture (the history of which is told by Michael Pollan, whom Webb ridiculously calls a "gourmand" and a "glutton"). Before that time, "organic food" was simply called "food." Similar comments apply to "free-range," "cage-free," "local produce," "hormone-free," and many other supposedly artificial devices of the cultural elite.

The theological justification Webb provides for ignoring the social impacts of our food choices is based on a notion that "Christianity secularized the production and consumption of food by taking the ritual out of animal sacrifices." It is, of

2. See Eric Schlosser, *Fast Food Nation: The Dark Side of the All-American Meal* (Boston: Houghton Mifflin, 2001).

course, true that Christianity did away with kosher laws and animal sacrifices. It does not follow, however, that food became a matter of spiritual and moral indifference to Christians. The idea that Judaism was crassly materialistic while Jesus came to preach a higher, more spiritual way has by now been entirely discredited by a whole generation of biblical scholars following E. P. Sanders and many others. The Eucharist becomes the sacrifice of Christians, and, at least at the beginning, a real meal was involved. There is no evidence in the biblical text for Webb's fanciful idea that Paul in 1 Corinthians 11:17–34 was especially concerned about those who "turned their noses up at the common fare of the lowest classes." Paul's concern, according to the text, was that those who had food refused to share it with those who had none. This is a failure to "discern the body," as Paul says, a failure to see that we must be concerned with the spiritual and material welfare of the weakest members of the body of Christ.

Webb grudgingly grants that "There is something to be said, then, for the argument that locally grown produce and humanely raised animal products capture and extend the moral message of Communion," but he says that such decisions should "flow naturally from acts of worshipping God" and not from "efforts to change the world" or attempts to "inject morality into our meals." I fail to see the usefulness of this sharp dichotomy between worship and morality. Of course, we should not substitute acts of consumption for the worship of God; Webb here is perhaps concerned, and rightly so, about the tendency of some churches to reduce being a Christian to morality, or of some churchgoers to substitute our own human actions in favor of social justice for acts of worship of the living God. But such distortions are simply the flip side of any dichotomy that demands that we choose worship instead of social justice. Paul does not seem to think that the material building up of the body of Christ in the world detracts from the worship of God; it is, rather, a manifestation of the work of the Holy Spirit in us.

In the latter part of his essay, Webb turns to my small book *Being Consumed* as an example of what goes wrong when food is regarded as having theological and moral import. I would like to respond to Webb's critiques, but I will need to distinguish where we disagree from where Webb has simply misread or misconstrued my text. To begin, Webb attributes to me the nonsensical idea that people "squander their money for no specific purpose." My point is not that people have no personal goals or ends; my point is that free market ideology (e.g., that of Milton Friedman) is indifferent to the goals that people choose for themselves, as long as those people get what they want. According to Friedman, economists have nothing to say about whether an economic transaction is good in some moral or theological sense; goodness is a matter left to individual morality. In economic matters we can only judge whether an exchange is free from external interference, not whether or not it is good. In the case of a Chinese factory worker making thirty cents an hour, the market is "free" if the employer and the employee enter voluntarily into the arrangement expecting to benefit: the employer boosts profitability, the employee staves off starvation. But this deliberate blindness to the grossly asymmetrical power relations involved cannot occlude the fact that economic transactions, as relations between people, are deeply moral (or immoral) and carry theological import. For this reason, I argue in my book that there is no "free market" as such to either criticize or praise. The real question to be answered with regard to each economic transaction is, "Is this transaction free?" That is, "Does it contribute to the flourishing of the people involved and the creation that sustains them? Does it contribute to the ultimate goal of all human life, which is participation in God?" Webb thinks it is too much to ask that mere purchases be invested with such theological import. I don't. I think that as long as some benefit from the cheap labor of others, Christians cannot declare such arrangements "secularized" and go on our merry way.[3]

If this is true, one cannot avoid—to the best that one's ability and resources allow—entering into hard, particular judgments about what kinds of economic arrangements are truly free. One example I give in my book is that of the Zweber farm, where my family has purchased grass-fed, organic meat. Webb raises skeptical questions about the slaughtering practices, price, and environmental impact at the Zweber farm. To answer these questions: the meat is butchered at Lorentz Meats in Cannon Falls, Minnesota, where a glass-walled abattoir allows those who so desire to watch the entire process (Pollan mentions Lorentz by name in his book *The Omnivore's Dilemma*[4]). The price is reasonable, because we buy in bulk and eliminate the supermarket. If we pay more, we do so voluntarily to support the Zwebers and their farm. *Pace* Webb, there are no "hidden costs" to the environment when meat is raised this way; cattle turn grass into high-quality protein. Little petroleum is required. Webb's final salvo at the Zwebers is that they are capitalists responding to a niche market. If successful, they or their competitors will inevitably go corporate, as consumers drive up demand and suppliers strive to cut costs. The irony here is that

3. See William T. Cavanaugh, *Being Consumed: Economics and Christian Desire* (Grand Rapids: Eerdmans, 2008).

4. Michael Pollan, *The Omnivore's Dilemma: A Natural History of Four Meals* (New York: Penguin, 2006).

Webb describes the "free" market in terms that are marked by a sense of inevitability and fatalism. If, however, people do not accept so-called free market ideology, and do not believe that their only role in the market is to maximize self-interest and lower costs to themselves, then there is nothing inevitable about the corporatization of the local food movement. Webb is right that consumers can help drive markets toward better products, but that only reinforces my point that we should use our economic power for good ends. Only when economic arrangements contribute to the true ends of the human person should we declare that market "free."

None of this implies, as Webb claims, that I think we should abandon the practice of private property; I explicitly invoke Thomas Aquinas's justification of private property on both page 29 and page 52 of my book. Neither do I suggest, as Webb claims, that all individuality is obliterated in the body of Christ; as I write, "At the same time, we do not lose our identities as unique persons, for as Paul says, each different member of the body is valued and needed for the body to function (1 Cor 12:12–27)" (55). Neither do I make the absurd claim that "The church should be in control of the market." Again, I will let my actual words from the book make the point: "The church is called to be a different kind of economic space and to foster such spaces in the world. This does not mean a 'sectarian' withdrawal from the world; Christians are in constant collaboration with non-Christians in making such spaces possible" (ix–x).

If Christians are attentive to our economic practices, we can help to create eucharistic spaces on earth that prefigure the fullness of the Babette's feast that God has prepared for us. This does not mean gluttony. Insofar as Webb's essay warns us against self-righteousness and self-indulgence, it is a salutary piece. Insofar as Webb encourages us to disregard the theological import of our practices of consumption, he is out to lunch.

4 A Response to William T. Cavanaugh's "Out to Lunch"

by STEPHEN H. WEBB

WHICH DOES THE EUCHARIST more closely resemble: a meal from Chez Panisse or McDonald's? The answer to that question seems obvious to me. One of the best restaurants in the world, Chez Panisse serves food that is organically, locally, and sustainably grown. Alice Waters started it in 1971, and it has become the holy shrine of progressive fine dining. It is to slow food what McDonald's is to fast. Chez Panisse started a revolution in how we think about food. How your ingredients are grown and where they come from is now as much a part of a good meal as its taste and presentation. McDonald's started a revolution too, but its goal seems to be to cram as many calories into the largest containers with the least amount of fiber possible. Nonetheless, McDonald's has become so successful that for many people it represents our daily bread: a burger and a Coke are for us today what bread and wine were for ordinary people in the time of Jesus. (The obvious difference is that people today think meat is necessary for a real meal whereas people in the ancient world treated meat as a luxury to be consumed infrequently and in moderation—except at banquets.) If the Eucharist is more like a simple and cheap meal than a slow and expensive one, then it resembles McDonald's more than Chez Panisse.

Here is another question: if Jesus were to come back today, which of these two restaurants would he be more likely to visit? You probably want to answer neither, but if he had to choose, the answer again seems obvious to me. McDonald's serves the ordinary folks in our society—from families in a hurry to people eating alone and from those on a tight budget to those who cannot get enough refills for their super-sized cups. The fare is not exactly healthy, but if you need a lot of calories for your dollar, it is the place to go. One french fry probably has more fat than an entire entrée at Chez Panisse, and you could eat at McDonald's for months (if your liver could stand it) for what you would pay for a single meal at the famous Berkeley establishment. Jesus would surely order a fish sandwich and not a burger, but just as surely he would hang out at McDonald's over Chez Panisse, where he would probably have a hard time getting a reservation anyway.

These were the kinds of points I was trying to make in my article about fast food and the Eucharist. The Eucharist was a simple meal of bread and wine. The Gospels do not mention any other items on the menu, and I have argued elsewhere that it is highly unlikely that meat was served at a meal that was focused on Jesus as the Lamb of God and thus the end of all animal sacrifices.[1] The "real" lamb would have been redundant and distracting. Jesus was giving of himself and had already, at the so-called cleansing of the temple, set himself up as the alternative to the temple sacrifices. He was facing death—it was "the night when he was betrayed" (1 Cor 11:23 NRSV)—and wanted to leave this meal behind as something the disciples could look forward to. The food was not the focus; he was. Every word he said was important, not every bite that was eaten. The meal would become the focus only when he was gone, and even then, the food (bread and wine) would need no special sauces to work its magic.

And that brings us to *Babette's Feast*. It is time to pay the check, tip the staff, turn off the lights, and leave that movie behind. I'm no Puritan (although even Puritans were not all that puritanical), but *Babette's Feast* has so many problems as a morally uplifting tale, let alone as an allegory of the Eucharist, that it is hard to know where to begin. Is this feast really "a symbol of Christ's self-emptying and Christ's call to the table of abundance," as William T. Cavanaugh contends?[2] Pagans at the time of Jesus (and since) certainly valued meals that took days to make, and many Christians today can practice gluttony in ways that would have made the Roman Emperors blush, but should Christians associate a lavish banquet with the abundance of grace? Even if Babette's banquet had a positive moral impact on those elderly, uptight Danes, can it have the same impact on those of us who live in North America? I don't think so. Much of the world is mired in obscene levels of poverty and starvation, while Americans have so much freedom from want that they can pick what sea their salt comes from. In other words, we already overinvest in the meaning of food. Why raise the

1. See Stephen H. Webb, *Good Eating* (Grand Rapids: Brazos, 2001) ch. 6: "The Lord's Supper as a Vegetarian Meal." I significantly expand on and modify this chapter in a forthcoming volume edited by Andy Alexis-Baker and Tripp York in the Peaceable Kingdom Series published by Cascade Books.

2. William T. Cavanaugh, "Out to Lunch," 14.

stakes even higher? We obsess over food because we crave community. We also long for novel and authentic experiences, whether they are in carefully re-created Italian gardens or cutting-edge premodern farms. Most of all, we like to feel morally good about the choices we make. We should be deeply suspicious, then, of how *Babette's Feast* encourages us to believe that our most extravagant pleasures can make the world a better place—that sensual excess and communal belonging can coincide. Babette has as little to do with the gospel as Alice Waters's cooking at Chez Panisse has to do with a late afternoon snack.

Remember the plot: Babette is fleeing counterrevolutionaries (conservatives!) and hiding out with an "austere Danish Christian sect."[3] If there were more austere Danes in the world, this film would have been accused of racism. Cavanaugh accuses me of being dualistic, but the film is a masterpiece of overdrawn, melodramatic dualism—the (female) sophisticated maker of taste versus the (mostly male) ethical rigorists who don't know a taste bud from a bedbug. Good and evil have not been further segregated since the time of the Manichaeans.

The only way to explain the enormous success of this film in religious studies and seminary classrooms is to see it as a self-serving prop of left-liberal criticism of conservative students. That is, professors who look down on their students as unsophisticated conservatives use this film (unconsciously, of course) as an allegory of their own teaching methods. When they show this film, they are really giving their students a visualization of how they, the professors, understand their own authority. The students are symbolized by the cruelly caricatured Calvinists—unreflective moral rigorists who have no taste for grand (French!) ideas or the finer things of life. The professor is obviously reflected in Babette, who is misunderstood by the reactionaries back home but finally has found a captive audience that she can woo with her underappreciated culinary skills. The students/Calvinists are supposed to be awed by Babette's/the professor's gift of great food/food for thought. Any criticism of the film is thus a matter of rudeness! How could you turn down a great meal? That would be like spitting in the face of an artist. Likewise, any criticism of the liberal professor who is trying to liberate Midwestern students from their unethical shopping trips to Walmart and Taco Bell would be ungrateful and ignorant. This film does not stomach any criticism—it literally leaves no room for careful evaluation, just as a meal at Chez Panisse leaves no room for dessert.

If we really wanted to help the poor in other countries, we would stop eating meat (which consumes more resources than other kinds of food) and go back to the

3. Ibid., 14.

kind of simple diet that the church fathers unanimously recommended. Take Tertullian, for example, who criticized those who spend too much time preparing and enjoying food: "For to you your belly is god, and your lungs a temple, and your paunch a sacrificial altar, and your cook the priest, and your fragrant smell the Holy Spirit, and your condiments spiritual gifts, and your belching prophecy." Or, if Tertullian is not to your liking, take Clement of Alexandria's advice: "We must guard against those articles of food which persuade us to eat when we are not hungry, bewitching the appetite. For is there not, within a temperate simplicity, a wholesome variety of eatables?"[4] Of course, much of the new food movement that Cavanaugh defends emphasizes simplicity, but it is a simplicity laboriously and artfully constructed. It is not the simplicity that comes from old-fashioned frugality.

So what is left of the disagreements I have with Cavanaugh? He thinks I deny "that food is sacramental."[5] I thought I was clear that the food of the Eucharist is sacramental, and all other food shares in that sacrament to the extent that it imitates that meal. He thinks I deny the power of consumer groups to accomplish moral change through establishing economic trends. On the contrary, I applaud such groups, but I attribute their very existence to the free market. Why isn't Cavanaugh also grateful for the freedom of the marketplace? He thinks I conflate "mere aestheticism with social justice," when, of course, that accurately describes his interest in good food. He thinks that raising cattle in the morally correct way involves no hidden costs. I think the production of meat has more hidden costs than any other consumer good ever made: the hidden life of the animal (the cost of life!), let alone all of the resources that animals consume (and vegetables do not) on their way to our dinner plates. He draws his dietary ethics from the popular writer Michael Pollan, and he thinks it is bizarre that I call Pollan a gourmand. Pollan is a secular writer who never talks about religion or Christianity, and he is famous for staging thirty-six-hour meals that he subsequently describes in the *New York Times*. With so many Christian theologians writing about diet these days, why would Cavanaugh want to take his inspiration from a self-confessed gourmand? He thinks my reading of 1 Corinthians is fanciful, but it is actually quite obvious. Read the passage: "When you come together, it is not really to eat the Lord's Supper. For when the time comes to eat, each of you goes ahead with your own supper, and one goes hungry and another becomes drunk. What! Do you not have homes to eat and drink in? Or do you show contempt for the church of God and humiliate those who have nothing? What should I say to you?

4. Quoted in Webb, *Good Eating*, 189–90.
5. Cavanaugh, "Out to Lunch," 14–15.

Should I commend you? In this matter I do not commend you!" (1 Cor 11:20–22 NRSV). Obviously, the wealthy were withholding food from the poor and abusing their privileges. Finally, he thinks I treat Judaism as crassly materialistic, which is not worth responding to.

What finally sets us apart is that Cavanaugh wants the economy to have a purpose, whereas I think that the purpose of the economy should be found outside of it. Cavanaugh jumps from the observation that "free-market ideology . . . is indifferent to the goals that people choose for themselves" to the conclusion that "goodness is a matter left to individual morality."[6] This is nonsense. Markets are highly regulated to ensure fairness, transparency, and honesty (not to mention taxes); just ask any businessperson. Only the most extreme libertarians (Friedman among them) hold the views that Cavanaugh attributes to me. Conservatives believe that the free market, in order to function properly, needs strong moral and religious traditions in addition to limited government regulation. That is why capitalism, Christianity, and democracy are so inextricably interconnected. Cavanaugh would untie those bonds by making the church itself a kind of polis. In his new book, he "argues for the church as a political body,"[7] just as in the book I discuss he argues for the church as a kind of "economic space" different from the market. This leads him to argue that "there is simply no alternative to the actual creation of cooperatives, businesses, and other organizations that behave according to the logic of the gospel." Such language suggests radical changes in democracy and capitalism, and he eagerly admits this: "The goal is indeed revolution, to transform the entirety of economic life into something worthy of God's children."[8] I think I trust Cavanaugh's good intentions, but I know I don't trust the unintended consequences that would result from them. The revolution he wants could not possibly occur according to the logic of anything other than an authoritarian government of some sort, which is why it is crucially important for all Christians to think deeply about how free markets, limited governments, and Christian faith fit so closely together.

6. Ibid., 17–18.

7. Cavanaugh, *Migrations of the Holy* (Grand Rapids: Eerdmans, 2011) 6.

8. Cavanaugh, *Being Consumed: Economics and Christian Desire* (Grand Rapids: Eerdmans, 2008) ix, x.

5 Digesting the Word:
A Triptych and Proposal on Dietary Choice

by DAVID GRUMETT

L AST JUNE, I WAS at a conference in the Romanian city of Constanța, the birthplace of monastic founder John Cassian. One day we drove inland from the Black Sea toward the Bulgarian border to visit some new and revived convents and monasteries, communities that have been swelling in size since the fall of Communism. We were on ancient Christian soil evangelized by Saint Andrew—who, the Orthodox love to remind Catholics, was the first of the apostles to acknowledge Jesus and the apostle who brought Peter to Jesus. Turning off the main road, we headed down a long bumpy track, past a desolate lake, until we stopped at a convent that housed about ten sisters, including the mother of our driver.

Foodwise, I am a pescatarian, so things had gone well for me so far—it was the Fast of the Apostles, the post-Pentecost fast that Christ called his disciples to undertake after he was taken from them (Matt 9:15; Mark 21:9–20; Luke 5:34–35), and for this reason, no red meat or poultry had been served to anyone during our trip—only vegetables, fruits, grains, and, on many days, seafood. And this fasting from red meat and poultry would continue through to the feast of Saints Peter and Paul at the end of the month. As we entered the small refectory, we were told with profuse apologies that this was a poor house which had adopted a fully vegetarian rule. With more notice the sisters might have been able to get us, as guests, some fish, but today all they had was vegetables.

The soup was, of course, delicious, its ingredients supplied from the fields and herb beds just outside. The obligatory tuică, a strong plum brandy, was also delicious. As in ancient Western monasteries, a little wine for the stomach wasn't frowned on, whereas meat was seen as more problematic. Indeed, the abbot hosting us even had his own wine label, which enabled him to follow Paul in prescribing his disciples something better for the stomach than mere water (1 Tim 5:23).

It was fortunate for us that Constanţa's most famous son, the monastic founder John Cassian, had, in his advice for monastic constitutions, seen fit to moderate the extreme asceticism he observed on his tour of Egypt and Palestine. At that time, competitions between hermits to see who could survive on the fewest chickpeas per month were not unknown, and two bread rolls a day, taken in the midafternoon, was considered a moderate diet.[1] Cassian's traveler's tales became the *Conferences*, compiled at the request of a French bishop to introduce Europeans to monastic practice. In his *Institutes*, Cassian cautions judiciously that "in our country neither the climate nor our own weakness could tolerate" such discipline.[2]

Yet his spiritual descendants in Constanţa and the wider Orthodox world have remained serious about dietary discipline. The Church requires abstinence from red meat and poultry for forty days before Christmas, two weeks prior to the Dormition, and of course during Lent, as well as for up to six weeks after the week of Pentecost as I mentioned earlier.[3] The rules for Lent are especially severe, with a mix of fasting, one meal a day, and uncooked food prescribed during the first and last weeks, depending on the strictness.[4]

An awareness of these rules, particularly when combined with direct experience of them, makes one see the lie in the common assumption that Orthodoxy is a vague spiritualism of icons, incense, and John Tavener. On the contrary, the fact that it has been able to preserve a level of discipline now almost totally lost in the West shows it to be conservative and moralizing. In this spiritual world, the Orthodox emphasis on mindful eating recognizes that the whole of the created order, including the physical body, is taken up into worship, just as spirituality makes direct material impact on daily life.

1. John Cassian, *Conferences*, trans. Colm Lubheid, Classics of Western Spirituality (Mahwah, NJ: Paulist, 1985) 2.19 (p. 77).

2. John Cassian, *The Institutes*, trans. Boniface Ramsey, Ancient Christian Writers 58 (Mahwah, NJ: Newman, 2000) 4.11 (p. 46).

3. Timothy Ware [*Also* Bishop Kallistos Ware of Diokleia], *The Orthodox Church*, new ed. (New York: Penguin, 1997) 300–301.

4. Kallistos Ware, "The Rules of Fasting," in *The Lenten Triodion* (London: Faber and Faber, 1978) 35–37.

It's no surprise that Pope Benedict XVI, so well attuned to historical theology and keen to promote Western spiritual renewal, has sought to remind Christians of the historical and spiritual importance of fasting. In his 2009 Lenten message, Benedict wrote the following:

> Fasting represents an important ascetical practice, a spiritual arm to do battle against every possible disordered attachment to ourselves. Freely chosen detachment from the pleasure of food and other material goods helps the disciple of Christ to control the appetites of nature, weakened by original sin, whose negative effects impact the entire human person.

Yet today, many Christians do not see fasting or abstinence as spiritually empowering. In his letter the pope continued,

> In our own day, fasting seems to have lost something of its spiritual meaning, and has taken on, in a culture characterized by the search for material well-being, a therapeutic value for the care of one's body. Fasting certainly bring benefits to physical well-being, but for believers, it is, in the first place, a "therapy" to heal all that prevents them from conformity to the will of God. In the Apostolic Constitution *Paenitemini* of 1966, the Servant of God Paul VI saw the need to present fasting within the call of every Christian to "no longer live for himself, but for Him who loves him and gave himself for him . . . he will also have to live for his brethren." Lent could be a propitious time to present again the norms contained in the Apostolic Constitution, so that the authentic and perennial significance of this long held practice may be rediscovered, and thus assist us to mortify our egoism and open our heart to love of God and neighbor, the first and greatest Commandment of the new Law and compendium of the entire Gospel.[5]

What then are the norms of *Paenitemini*? Pope Benedict did not recite them, despite urging bishops to present them anew. Presumably they know them by heart, but if you don't, then here goes: Meat should not be eaten on any Friday, excepting days of obligation, although eggs, milk products, and animal fat are allowed.

---

5. Pope Benedict XVI, "Message of His Holiness Benedict XVI for Lent 2009," December 11, 2008, http://www.vatican.va/holy_father/benedict_xvi/messages/lent/documents/hf_ben-xvi_mes_20081211_lent-2009_en.html.

During Lent, complete fasting is required on Ash Wednesday and Good Friday, which means that only one full meal is allowed on each of these days, though a little food is permitted in the morning and evening. In all cases, abstinence from meat is obligatory from age fourteen and fasting is obligatory from age twenty-one, with both obligations continuing until age sixty.[6]

In Western liberal consumer society, no one is used to being told what to eat. But let's be mindful of the rigors enforced in former times. In Britain, meat eating during Lent was outlawed by royal decree until the 1660s—well over a century after the Reformation—with infringements punishable by fine or imprisonment.[7] Dairy products and eggs were also prohibited during Lent until the 1530s, which is where the custom of giving eggs as gifts at Easter originates—if you had 200 eggs going spare, what else would you give as a present?

In comparison to these laws, then, *Paenitemini* is very modern in the low levels of meat abstinence it demands: just Fridays and Ash Wednesday. And the most obvious difference between *Paenitemini* and religious dietary guidelines of the sixteenth and seventeenth century is the absence of any requirement to restrict one's diet during Lent. In the background seems to be an outdated assumption that in order to survive people must eat meat.

The English Reformation monarchs took dietary discipline far more seriously, enforcing Wednesdays, Fridays, and Saturdays, as well as the whole of Lent, as meat-free, yet they were excommunicated for their troubles. Indeed, in medieval and Reformation England more than half the days of the year were days of abstinence from meat: Lent, Advent, Fridays, Wednesdays, Saturdays, and the eves of the major saints' days. Days of abstention outnumbered days of unbridled consumption.

We now know that unrestrained consumption does more bad than good for body and society. Christians in the West should seriously consider not only adopting some kind of an abstinence regiment, but also advancing beyond the rules of *Paenitemini* by reappraising what they eat, where it comes from, its social and economic justice impacts, and its carbon footprint. Furthermore, given current levels of longevity and health care, there is no longer any reason to limit this invitation to

6. Pope Paul VI, "Apostolic Constitution *Paenitemini* of the Supreme Pontiff Paul VI on Fast and Abstinence," February 17, 1966, http://www.vatican.va/holy_father/paul_vi/apost_constitutions/documents/hf_p-vi_apc_19660217_paenitemini_en.html. Note that these requirements may be modified by regional bishops' conferences.

7. David Grumett and Rachel Muers, *Theology on the Menu: Asceticism, Meat and Christian Diet* (New York: Routledge, 2010) 28. Remarkably, no previous systematic study has been completed of dietary legislation and its enforcement, despite extensive source material.

people who are under the age of sixty. Disciplined use of natural resources and of our own bodies, as temples of the Spirit, needs to be rebuilt into Christian cultural, social, political, and ethical consciousness.

~

In present Western secular society, there is a rapidly growing awareness of the many problems that result from dietary indiscipline. Globally, livestock production generates a higher proportion of the world's greenhouse gases (18 percent) than motor transport (13 percent). Livestock produce high proportions of the total global volume of noxious gases, including 35–40 percent of the methane, which is 23 times more effective at trapping heat than carbon dioxide, and 64 percent of nitrous oxide, which is 296 times more effective than carbon dioxide. Thirteen million hectares of forest are cleared annually to provide land for grazing or feed crops, reducing global carbon storage capacity and destroying soil structure, which leads to desertification, thereby perpetuating ecological decline.[8]

Furthermore, poor diet is a leading contributor to many of our most widespread health problems. These include cancer, heart disease, hypertension, diabetes, and premature death. And whereas the hallmark cause of a poor diet in the United States used to be insufficient food intake, it is now excessive consumption and bad dietary choices. These poor dietary decisions have a massive economic impact, with obesity alone estimated to have costs the public purse $147 billion in medical expenditures in 2008[9]—this is at a time of public spending cuts, tax increases, and rising health insurance premiums.

Looking further afield, over 900 million people worldwide are malnourished out of a global population of 6.8 billion,[10] yet even in the regions most affected by malnourishment, land is expropriated from local communities to produce foods that are sent to the developed world. Likewise, massive quantities of crops are grown solely for the purpose of feeding animals that are then slaughtered to be eaten by the affluent. These areas of land and crops could easily be used to feed undernourished humans if global levels of meat consumption were cut and Western supermarkets

8. Henning Steinfeld et al., *Livestock's Long Shadow: Environmental Issues and Options* (Rome: Food and Agriculture Organization of the United Nations, 2006).

9. E. A. Finkelstein, J. G. Trogdon, J. W. Cohen, and W. Dietz, "Annual Medical Spending Attributable to Obesity: Payer- and Service-Specific Estimates," *Health Affairs* 28 (2009) 822–31.

10. Food and Agriculture Organization of the United Nations, *The State of Food Insecurity in the World 2008: High Food Prices and Food Security—Threats and Opportunities* (Rome: FAO, 2008).

stocked more modestly. But, in fact, the opposite is happening. Meat consumption is soaring in East Asia, precisely the part of the world where the majority of malnourished people live. Food cultures there have traditionally not relied on meat, but it is now seen as a status symbol and as a signifier of membership in the developed world. Not much has changed since the eighteenth century, when in England the ability of the yeoman class to put meat on the family table was based on enclosure of common land, economic superiority, and implicit violence. These objectives are now being pursued by ever more people in the world, but they self-evidently cannot be attained by everybody.

Others might be persuaded of the need for renewed dietary discipline by the fact that obesity is now regularly cited as a national security threat—because increasingly weighty numbers of Americans would fail to meet the minimum enrollment standard for military service.[11] After all, not even Winston Churchill was upbeat enough to proclaim, "We shall fight on the beaches, we shall fight on the landing grounds, we shall fight in the fields and in the streets, we shall fight in the burger joint." Though he didn't get out much on Saturday nights.

Because of these reasons and others, the dietary reform movement is currently gaining major impetus from ecologists, health reformers, global justice advocates, and even the homeland security agenda. As ever more people discover that the global meat economy emits more pollution than cars, is killing hundreds of millions of people prematurely, wastes natural resources, and diverts food from far needier fellow humans, we should at the very least be able to agree that meat-eating levels must be reduced urgently and drastically.

Around us we see little more than scattered shards of past Christian attempts to change dietary choices. Peanut butter and breakfast cereals, including the Kellogg's and Weetabix brands, were initially developed by Seventh Day Adventists to wean consumers off their pork, beans, and pie breakfasts.[12] Yet most Christians are happy to turn a blind eye to the fact that undisciplined food consumption is at the root of many pressing social and political problems.

11. Rochelle Nolte, Shawn C. Franckowiak, Carlos J. Crespo, and Ross E. Andersen, "United States Military Weight Standards: What Percentage of US Young Adults Meet the Current Standards?," *American Journal of Medicine* 113 (2002) 486–90.

12. Daniel Sack, *Whitebread Protestants: Food and Religion in American Culture* (New York: St. Martin's, 2001); and Gerald Carson, *Cornflake Crusade* (New York: Rinehart, 1957).

One might suppose that the Eucharist provides Christians with all the theological resources needed to take food seriously. From a vegetarian standpoint, because it uses bread and wine, the Eucharist could be viewed as marking a clean break with the practice of animal sacrifice. Moreover, by making a dining ritual central to our collective life, we might be presumed to be promoting dietary discipline as a key spiritual concern. Yet in reality, the Eucharist has made an ambiguous impact on Christian dietary discipline, often transposing discussions about food, dining, and fellowship into a realm of theological symbolism far removed from the concrete realities of everyday food choices. In the liturgical meal, images of feasting, consumption, sharing, hospitality, and justice abound, but they are typically abstracted from their most obvious concrete context, that of real, everyday food consumption.

Perhaps Christians need to look to nonliturgical sources for constructive material to shape a new spiritual understanding of food. In church tradition, food has been a central shaper and signifier of people and communities. In religious experience, fasting has provoked dreams, visions, and prophecies, while feasting has brought Christians together to celebrate Easter and Christmas. Food has helped build the cornerstones of Christian doctrine, with creation, the fall, the incarnation, salvation, and redemption all occurring through food: the plants and fruit trees given by God to humans and animals for food; the fruit of the tree of the knowledge of good and evil eaten by Adam; Christ as second Adam, offering his body as bread to reverse that fault; Christ as lamb of God on the cross, fulfilling the requirements of the Passover sacrifice; the Eucharist of bread and wine, Christ's body and blood, shared to form the Church.

The most obvious source to revisit, however, would seem to be Scripture. In the Old Testament gluttony is the first sin, committed by Adam and Eve in the garden of Eden; it is the sin that many early Christian interpreters, including Cassian and Gregory the Great, believed all other sins, including lust, followed.[13] And there is a lot of fasting and abstinence from meat in Scripture. Israel fasted on manna in the wilderness and later before defeating the Amalekites. Moses fasted on the mountain where he received the Commandments. Hannah fasted before giving birth to Samuel. Israel fasted before and after subduing the Philistines. David hid from Saul in the desert and, as Psalm 63 implies, fasted. Elijah was fed by ravens in the desert. Even King Ahab fasted to postpone judgment on his house. King Hezekiah fasted and the Lord struck down the Assyrian army. Daniel and his friends ate vegetables and water in the court of King Nebuchadnezzar with the result that they "looked healthier

13. William Ian Miller, "Gluttony," *Representations* 60 (1997) 92–112.

and better nourished than any of the young men who ate the royal food," gaining knowledge and prophetic insight. Jesus himself fasted forty days in the desert, then resisted the temptation to turn stones into bread to ease his desperate hunger. Anna fasted in the temple, where she saw the child Jesus and prophesied about him. John the Baptist ate locusts and wild honey in the wilderness, or something similar. Jesus ate with his disciples as well as with outcasts, and he cooked and ate fish to prove his bodily resurrection. John the Baptist was killed during a banquet and his head put on a serving dish. Paul fasted several times.[14] Given food's ubiquity in Scripture, it is unsurprising that biblical scholars are currently doing much to put food issues onto the Christian menu.[15] Theologians need to pay attention to their work and allow Scripture's literal concern with food to permeate their own reflection more deeply.

In a society of continual, undifferentiated provision, the material texturing of life fades into the background. But basic needs were formerly met far more precariously; these needs were under constant threat of disruption by weather, war, pestilence, or disease. Changing availability of food was the norm, and this was the backdrop against which theologians and churchmen legislated, exhorted, and interpreted. Maybe we need to work harder today to realize how great a gift our food is, though our imaginations should find much to feed on when contemplating climate change and global poverty.

To take diet seriously, however, Christians need to take a look beyond their own tradition to what is happening in secular society. Historically, food discipline was enforced by both church rules and civil law—people were not simply more pious than we are today—but it would be difficult for the church and state to be so interventionist today with regard to our diets. Is that necessary though? Millions are gaining a new interest in diet as a key to personal spirituality, often without any institutional religious commitment. Today, so much more can be achieved by shaping personal choice than by compulsion. People are discovering the truth of Michel Foucault's intuition that dietary discipline, far from being a denial of the self and its flourishing, is a way of standing out from the masses, asserting personal identity,

14. See Gen 3; Exod 16:3, 17:3, 34:28; Deut 9:9, 9:18; 1 Sam 1:7–8, 7:6, 14:24, 23:14b; Ps 63:1b; 1 Kgs 17:6, 21:27–29; 2 Kgs 19:1; Dan 1:12–17; Matt 3:4b, 9:9–13; Mark 1:6, 2:13–17; Luke 2:36–38, 24:41–43; John 21:9–13; and 2 Cor 11:27.

15. E.g., John M. G. Barclay, "Food, Christian Identity and Global Warming: A Pauline Call for a Christian Food Taboo," *Expository Times* 121 (2010) 585–93; Nathan MacDonald, *Not Bread Alone: The Uses of Food in the Old Testament* (New York: Oxford University Press, 2008); and David G. Horrell, *Solidarity and Difference: A Contemporary Reading of Paul's Ethics* (New York: T. & T. Clark, 2005) 166–203.

and taking control of one's destiny.[16] Christians need to connect with these new currents of reflective material living that are ever more prominent beyond church walls. We need to recognize with penitence that it is perhaps our own doctrines that have caused us to become disconnected from real, material daily life, and we need to recognize that this renewed interest in reflective material living in secular society in fact manifests an aspect of Christian tradition that we ourselves need to recover, like the Israelites seeking and receiving the treasures of their Egyptian neighbors in order to journey with them out of Egypt (Exod 3:21–22 and 12:35–36).

Christians also need to look at diet as an interfaith issue. I shall end by reflecting on this by way of a fabulous painting, Diego Velázquez's *Christ in the House of Mary and Martha*, which was chosen for the cover of my recent book, *Theology on the Menu: Asceticism, Meat, and Christian Diet* (Routledge, 2010). In the painting, Velázquez portrays with great realism a woman standing at a kitchen table preparing a meal. On the table are garlic, a red chili, an egg, and a fish. It looks like she's making aioli. Her creased puffy cheeks betray that she's upset. Slaving away to make the supper as her strong arms have done so many times before, she looks resigned to her work, continued faithfully while others gain public recognition or enjoy spiritual contemplation. In the background sits Christ with the pious Mary seated lovingly at his feet gazing up into his face and feasting on his words, while Martha approaches from behind protesting Mary's failure to do her share of the household chores. We may suppose that the woman in the kitchen is Martha herself, suggestive of other maids who labor to support and feed households.

Velázquez was of Jewish *converso* lineage—in other words, he was from a Spanish Jewish family who had converted to Catholicism under strong pressure and the threat of expulsion if they refused. This religious heritage helps explain his interest in food and spirituality. Yet the dish being prepared is not distinctively Jewish. The painting, produced during Velázquez's Seville period, would undoubtedly have gotten him in trouble with the authorities of the aggressively Catholic kingdom of Castile had it represented some element of the Passover meal. So Velázquez's Jewish heritage is veiled—the simple fact of his portraying a kitchen, food, and meal preparation, topics standardly viewed as spiritually significant in the Jewish tradition but less so in Christianity, makes his heritage somewhat apparent.[17] But because of this, he puts food into a Christian context.

16. Michel Foucault, *Security, Territory, Population: Lectures at the Collège de France, 1977–78*, ed. Michel Senellart, trans. Graham Burchell (New York: Palgrave Macmillan, 2007) esp. 205–8.

17. An excellent discussion of this image is in Jane Boyd and Philip S. Esler, *Visuality and Biblical*

In Western societies, food rules have often been associated with "other" religions. In our current pluralist age this perception has, if anything, grown. The Muslim who avoids pork or the vegetarian Hindu might once have been viewed as representing exotic foreign lands, with their food habits heightening the mystique projected onto such places. But members of "other" religions are now certainly people with whom Christians live in close proximity and people with whom we might well share hospitality. These interactions present Christians with opportunities to learn how elements of material life might be central to religious identity and to thereby recover aspects of their own faith tradition.

More specifically, an awareness of the importance attached to food in other religions, such as shown by Velázquez, as well as in Pope Paul VI's *Paenitemini* and daily Orthodox practice, makes us recognize that a proper appraisal of the place of food in Christian spirituality is a pressing matter. It reminds us of one of the implications of the Christian doctrine of the incarnation: that, in taking physical human form, God in Christ brought the whole of material reality into his presence. This makes the whole of the material world, including food and diet, deeply relevant to corporate Christian living and personal spirituality.

Text: Interpreting Velázquez' Christ with Martha and Mary as a Test Case, Arte e archeologia 26 (Florence: L. S. Olschki, 2004). Yet not even here is the significance of its painter's religious ambiguity identified.

6 To Love Oneself through Food: Geneen Roth and a Christian Resistance to Compulsive Eating

by ELIZABETH L. ANTUS

AS THEY STRIVE FOR slenderness, many women in the United States express lifelong frustration with food and their own bodies. Every reader of this piece, if she herself does not experience frustration at her own body shape and size, likely knows at least one woman who chronically diets, expresses displeasure at her thighs and stomach, and hopes for that sunny day that she can lose some amount of weight so that she can go on vacation or fit into a certain dress. It is commonplace for young girls to scrutinize their thighs, waist, and arms as they wish to sculpt and trim themselves according to the airbrushed images they see in advertising. This pressure affects women of all different kinds of body sizes—constant disapproval of one's body is a staple of North American womanhood.[1]

This fixation on losing weight results in dangerously *underweight* bodies, as women diet and exercise obsessively. Ten million US women now suffer from anorexia and/or bulimia, and at least half of them admit to feeling dissatisfied with their body size. The economic success of the almost wholly ineffective diet industry, now worth almost $70 billion a year, reflects this dissatisfaction. This dieting

1. In focusing on women's struggles with body image in this piece, I do not deny that men also struggle with health and bodily self-acceptance. Men now make up approximately 10 percent of those who struggle with eating disorders in the United States. However, given that women still statistically outpace men ten to one in terms of eating disorders and other kinds of bodily dissatisfaction, this piece focuses on women. See Sharlene Nagy Hesse-Biber, *The Cult of Thinness*, 2nd ed. (New York: Oxford University Press, 2007) 188–226. For more on the power dynamics at play in the push for thinness upon and by women in the United States, see Sylvia K. Blood, *Body Work: The Social Construction of Women's Body Image* (New York: Routledge, 2005) 50. Also see Carla Rice, "How Big Girls Become Fat Girls: The Cultural Production of Problem Eating and Physical Inactivity," in *Critical Feminist Approaches to Eating Dis/orders*, eds. Helen Malson and Maree Burns (New York: Routledge, 2009) 97–109.

obsession also indirectly contributes to the epidemic of dangerously *overweight* bodies as many women fail at dieting and then succumb to unhealthy overconsumption. When they quit their diets, they quickly gain back all the weight they lost and then some. Thus, as we continue to idealize female thinness with full force and vigor, women struggle with fatness more than ever.[2]

Christians cannot afford to dismiss many women's fraught relationship with food and their own bodies as a sort of trite gender niche issue fit only for talk shows; this phenomenon is a spiritual crisis that should spur the deepest reflection of Christians upon the meaning of the life, death, and resurrection of Jesus. Given the complexity of the problem, I will explore only one dimension of it in this essay: women's practices of compulsive eating, namely, eating that is not about nourishment of the body through the proportionate intake of food but, rather, about either shrinking the body by dieting or expanding the body by bingeing.[3] We cannot theologically analyze the trends toward eating disorders and obesity until we take an uncomfortably close-up look at what happens to women when they believe their only choices for happiness are through dieting or bingeing. We cannot reform society's views toward food and the female body until we understand what is happening to women in the details of their everyday lives. To this end, I engage with the work of "spiritual but not religious" best-selling nonfiction writer Geneen Roth, in particular her 2010 *Women, Food and God*, to argue two points: first, that eating practices and

2. When I speak about *underweight* and *overweight* bodies, I am using these terms in relation to body mass index (BMI) measurements. For women, *underweight* signifies having a BMI of less than 18.5 percent, *standard* signifies having a BMI of 18.5—24.9 percent, *overweight* signifies having a BMI of 25.0—29.9 percent, and *obese* signifies having a BMI of at least 30 percent. See "Calculate Your Body Mass Index," National Heart, Lung, and Blood Institute, http://www.nhlbi.nih.gov/. For anorexia and bulimia statistics, see Hesse-Biber, *The Cult of Thinness*, 3–15. For diet failure rates (which are about 95 percent), see "Why Diets Fail," http://www.healthy-diet-habits.com/why-diets-fail.html; and "News Briefs: Statistics/Trends," http://www.healthyweightnetwork.com/trends.htm. For obesity statistics, see "Statistics Related to Overweight and Obesity," Weight-Control Information Network, http://win.niddk.nih.gov/statistics/#overweight. The obesity epidemic in the United States is certainly complex; it is deeply related to North Americans' increasingly sedentary lifestyle as well as our increasingly caloric and fatty food. In this piece, however, I focus on the socio-aesthetic pressures around women's bodies. For more on these other factors, see Tara Parker-Pope, "Less Active at Work, Americans Have Packed on Pounds," *New York Times*, May 25, 2011; as well as Hesse-Biber, *The Cult of Thinness*, 23–24.

3. Not all women who struggle with health are compulsive eaters. Compulsive eating is a kind of addiction affecting a certain subset of people, and other people pick other addictions to create numbness when life is too painful. See Geneen Roth, *Women, Food and God: An Unexpected Path to Almost Everything* (New York: Scribner 2010), 52. I also think that Roth's constructive points about food awareness apply more broadly to anybody who wishes to cultivate the best possible relationship with food and her own body.

fundamental religious beliefs are profoundly interconnected realities, and second, that practiced respect for the body is indispensable for women attempting to confront their emotional and spiritual pain.

THE GENEEN ROTH STORY

Geneen Roth has written and lectured about food and the female body for decades. Her determination to help women stems from her own struggle with food, dieting, and her body. As a child, Roth sought sanctuary from her parents' tumultuous marriage by overeating privately.[4] She subsequently became convinced that her weight problem had caused her parents' strife, and she commenced a slough of dieting regiments. For Roth, bingeing and dieting served important, mutually reciprocal functions in her life: "I started dieting the same year I started bingeing," she explains, "Dieting gave me a purpose. Bingeing gave me relief from the relentless attempt to be someone else."[5] Bingeing provided Roth an escape from the pain and loneliness of her life, and dieting then provided a channel for guilty self-reform. And back and forth. She undertook a decades-long foray into the world of dieting, in which she attempted the All-Grape-Nuts diet, became addicted to laxatives and amphetamines, and spent months in a sugar-crazed haze of bingeing. She varied in weight from a mere eighty pounds to uncomfortably overweight.[6] Roth thus spent the first half of her life gaining and losing over one thousand pounds.

At her breaking point, she made a desperate choice. Exhausted by the grind of the binge-diet cycle and seriously contemplating suicide, Roth decided that, instead of killing herself, she would stop dieting and simply accept herself as very overweight (which she was at that time). This decision marked the beginning of a new form of self-relation, and as a byproduct, she did eventually arrive at her natural weight.

Roth's story is important not because she definitively lost weight, but because she stopped trying to fix and numb herself through dieting and bingeing. She underwent a dramatic spiritual transformation in her attitude toward her body, and it is this shift in body praxis, not Roth's weight loss per se, that I encourage women struggling with food and weight to consider. Although Roth espouses a religiously eclectic perspective, her claims regarding the spiritual valence of eating and the

4. Roth, *Women, Food and God*, 21–24.

5. Ibid., 23.

6. Ibid., 13.

body as a site of dignified self-knowing freshly crystallize the fundamental insights of Christian anthropology.[7]

GOD IS IN THE FOOD

Roth breathes new life into the Christian belief that food and the act of eating are deeply connected to God. Christians harbor a fundamental belief that God intended us to take joy in the goodness of creation and the body. The Gospels are shot through with tableaux of Jesus feasting with the poor and the outcast as well as parables in which he compares the inclusive graciousness of God to a wedding banquet (Matt 15:32–39 and 22:1–14; Mark 6:34–44; and Luke 14:1–24).[8] Eating with diverse members of society punctuates Jesus's life at crucial junctures: breaking bread with the disciples before his death, he says, "I have eagerly desired to eat this Passover with you before I suffer" (Luke 22:14–20); and, in John, he catches fish with them on the beach after his resurrection and says, "Come, have breakfast" (John 21:1–14). Womanist, feminist, and liberation theologians have employed these kinds of passages to point out that Christians are called, in following Jesus, to break bread with all people, especially those who are impoverished or considered unlovable in society.[9] I want to add that the Gospels also call Christians, in imitation of Jesus, to nourish themselves and each other with food. Eating thus mediates God's intentions about the concrete shape of human flourishing in the everyday. The Gospels do not suggest that a woman needs to make herself thin through the restriction of food or that she should best enjoy food through bingeing on it. They portray God as wanting the ongoing nourishment of all and the occasional celebratory feasting of all. This depiction of the spiritual dimension of eating matters for the food crisis many women in America are experiencing.

Partaking of food constitutes a spiritual praxis not only at public, celebratory feasts, but also when one woman, any woman, sits by herself with something like a

---

7. Ibid., 13–14, 28, 58–59, and 108–10. Roth began helping women with food and weight after she decided to stop dieting and bingeing but before she lost weight, and even after she lost weight she still struggled deeply with appreciation for her body; being thinner did not somehow cure her of her suffering. Roth's epiphany thus encompasses more than the mere loss of weight.

8. All allusions to and quotations from Scripture are from the NAB.

9. See M. Shawn Copeland, *Enfleshing Freedom: Body, Race, and Being* (Minneapolis: Fortress, 2010) 61–62. See also Elizabeth A. Johnson, *She Who Is: The Mystery of God in Feminist Theological Discourse* (New York: Crossroad, 2007 [1992]) 157–58; and Jon Sobrino, *Jesus the Liberator: A Historical-Theological Reading of Jesus of Nazareth* (Maryknoll, NY: Orbis, 1994) 102–4.

plate of spaghetti and contemplates whether she can resist the compulsive urges to binge or restrict. When women are unable to use food simply to nourish and take pleasure in their bodies out of gratitude to God because they struggle with food compulsion, it deeply concerns God and all that God desires for them. Roth captures this truth in her descriptions of what happens inside the minds of women as they make decisions about eating—whether women acknowledge it or not, how they explicitly choose to consume reveals their implicit beliefs about the value of their life and its potential connection to joy and peace:

> Our relationship to food is an exact microcosm of our relationship to life itself. I believe we are walking, talking expressions of our deepest convictions; everything we believe about love, fear, transformation and God is revealed in how, when, and what we eat. . . . If we are interested in finding out what we actually believe . . . we need go no further than the food on our plates. . . . God—however we define him or her—is on our plates.[10]

How a woman eats every day expresses her real beliefs about whether she is loved—by God and by others—or not. God is in the cake, the cornflakes, and the broccoli.

Roth suggests that women eat compulsively (that is, when they are not hungry) because they believe at a deep and often unexamined level that they are fundamentally damaged, that they are consequently devoid of love and peace, and that food is therefore the best source of security they can procure for themselves in the moment. Food becomes a focal point, a sanctuary, when compulsive eaters believe their lives are intolerable, or they are grieving for the death of a family member, or they have been laid off, or they are unmarried—or married—and lonely. Roth states, "Compulsive eating is an attempt to avoid the absence (of love, of comfort, knowing what to do) when we find ourselves in the desert of a particular moment, feeling, situation."[11] Compulsive eating keeps feelings of abandonment and despair at bay, and even when compulsive eaters experience happiness, they still want to overeat because overeating has already been encoded as happiness and security. In this vein, Roth suggests that a woman who consistently overfills her plate and consumes to the point of feeling sick probably believes that the world is hostile and isolating, and that she must stock up on food as her only real source of comfort.[12]

10. Roth, *Women, Food and God*, 2.

11. Ibid., 34.

12. Ibid., 17.

Some women then recognize their bingeing tendencies and become so scared of being out of control, especially if other areas of their lives feel out of control, that they swing in the opposite direction and dive headfirst into dieting regimes. A woman who chronically restricts the food on her plate probably believes that the particular agonies of her existence will be manageable if she can control what she is allowed to intake.[13] In particular, she believes her dietary self-discipline will compensate for her fundamental sense of being damaged or abandoned—if she can punish herself into shape, she can manage the rest of her life, and she will then be worthy of love. In explaining the mindset of women who feel this way, Roth explains that "being thin becomes The Test. Losing weight becomes their religion. They must suffer humiliation and torment, they must enroll in an endless succession of dietary privations, and then and only then will they be pure, be holy, be saved."[14] Through diet, these women believe they will come ever closer to approximating the cultural image of the perfectly tailored, trim, and elegant woman.

For Roth, food compulsion mediated either through bingeing or dieting ultimately fails because it is an abuse of the physical to address emotional and spiritual pain women believe they are incapable of facing head-on. In this way, compulsive eaters try to shrink themselves to fit inside their fixation on food, and they make their precious lives narrow and joyless: "By collapsing the whole of our wanting into something as tangible as butterscotch pudding, we cancel poetry, sacredness, longing from our lives and resign ourselves to living with hearts banged shut. . . . We don't want to *eat* hot fudge sundaes as much as we want our lives to *be* hot fudge sundaes."[15] When women believe they are not worthy of experiencing interior peace and delight within the actual ambit of their everyday lives, they either fixate on the momentary joy of food or gain composure through the denial of food. For Roth, then, the question becomes: how can women learn to use food as a way to express a sense of fundamental lovability with themselves, others, and God?

Unlike some Christian figures who have tinkered with the connection between weight and spirituality in alarming ways, Roth is *not* claiming that fatness is an iniquity for which women are entirely culpable and need to get over as they battle their "demons."[16] To the contrary, Roth believes that we need to get beyond our yearning

13. Ibid., 31.

14. Ibid., 64.

15. Ibid., 172, 174.

16. Presbyterian minister Charlie Shedd made this argument in 1957 with his Christian diet book *Pray Your Weight Away* (Philadelphia: Lippincott, 1957). These kinds of arguments have continued in

for thin bodies and our stigmatizing of fat ones and instead think more about how each person, with her particular body size and shape, can care for her own body. Roth is thus shifting the interconnection of weight and spirituality away from the illusory, ever-shifting image of the Thin Woman and toward the learned praxis of embodied self-care that must be tailored to each person of any size. It does not matter if a woman weighs 120 pounds: if she eats compulsively through bingeing or dieting, she needs to take an honest look at her food conduct and can potentially benefit from Roth's insights.[17] Conversely, a woman may technically be classified as overweight for a variety of reasons related to overall health, genetics, and age, but if she exhibits the kind of embodied praxis of self-care that Roth ultimately articulates, then her praxis and her body are to be celebrated and respected. Overall, then, Roth's paradigm shift allows women to contemplate how to be kind to themselves and to value their bodies, rather than punish themselves for the supposed sin of flabbiness.

THE FLESH

Roth deepens Christian thinking about the goodness of the body. Christians have always labored to articulate the goodness of the body as created by God and redeemed through Jesus. Christian theologians today, especially feminist and liberationist theologians such as M. Shawn Copeland, Elizabeth Johnson, and Jon Sobrino, among many others, have insisted on the inherent dignity of the body against various kinds of philosophical dualisms that attempt in varying ways to identify the essence of the human person with the immaterial soul, spirit, or mind and then to relativize or belittle the body as something inferior and ultimately transient. One can see the patristic theologian Augustine of Hippo struggling with his Neoplatonic and Stoic inheritance, and his deep suspicion of the female body and of sexuality in general, as he tried to hold in tension the goodness of the body with his desire to gain eternal life and slough off the body as "corruptible."[18] This permutation of suspicion toward the body runs deep in the Christian tradition and eventually intersects with modern Cartesian dualism, which frames the body as a kind of objectified and mechanized *res extensa* that merely facilitates the mind's engagement with the world.[19]

different forms up through the present. Popular now is the Weigh Down Diet and the Slim for Him programs that fixate on weight loss as necessary to becoming closer to Jesus.

17. Roth, *Women, Food and God*, 52.

18. Tarsicius Jan Van Bavel, "'No One Ever Hated His Own Flesh': Eph. 5:29 in Augustine," *Augustiniana* 45.1–2 (July 1995) 45–93.

19. The Christian tradition displays a striking level of complexity regarding attitudes toward the

Practices of sanitizing, domesticating, and distancing the body are not only in the past, nor are they a problem only for philosophers and theologians. In her analysis of compulsive bingeing and dieting, Roth identifies an insidious form of dualism in the body hatred of women who wish to trim, tailor, tuck, suck, sculpt, deprive, or overstuff their bodies as they live out their compulsive relationship with food. This kind of dualistic self-identity plays out in different ways depending on whether a woman diets or binges.

First, Roth explains that dieting, as a desperate lifestyle choice in which one chooses to apply a heteronomous code of eating rules upon one's body, falsely presupposes that the body is unruly and cannot be trusted. Dieting is a doomed practice that creates more frustration because, through it, women attempt to fix whatever they think is deeply wrong with themselves, namely, their bodies.[20] But even if they lose weight and shrink down to their goal weight, they realize that being thin does not take away their fundamental sense of unhappiness with their bodies. Even though women continue to diet, it cannot make good on its promise of peace:

> We don't want to be thin because thinness is inherently life-affirming or lovable or healthy. If this were true, there would be no tribes in Africa in which women are fat and regal and long-lived. There would be no history of matriarchies in which women's fecundity and sheer physical abundance were worshipped. We want to be thin because thinness is the purported currency of happiness and peace and contentment in our time. And although that currency is a lie . . . most systems of weight loss fail because they don't live up to their promise: weight loss does not make people happy. . . . Even a wildly successful diet is a colossal failure because inside the new body is the same sinking heart.[21]

body, but it is outside the scope of this paper to trace all of these strands or to explain why many Christians have harbored such a suspicion toward the body. For insight into the impact of Cartesianism on the body in modernity, see Charles Taylor, *Sources of the Self: The Making of Modern Identity* (Cambridge, MA: Harvard University Press, 1989) 143–76. For a thorough rendering of early Christian attitudes toward the body, see Peter Brown, *The Body and Society: Men, Women, and Sexual Renunciation in Early Christianity*, Lectures on the History of Religions, n.s., 13 (New York: Columbia University Press, 1988). For a macrocosmic overview of Christian attitudes toward the body and sexuality throughout the Christian tradition, see Elizabeth A. Dreyer, *Earth Crammed with Heaven: A Spirituality of Everyday Life* (New York: Paulist, 1994) 114–35.

20. Roth, *Women, Food and God*, 83.

21. Ibid., 176–77.

Many women have come to believe that once they are thin, their lives will be manageable and they will suddenly be eminently deserving of love, success, and attention. But here is the thing: when women do not respect their bodies as they are, *before dieting*, becoming thin cannot manufacture that self-respect out of thin air. Once thin, women will still feel empty, fragile, bored, and lonely. The praxis of self-hatred will never produce a state of self-love.[22] Furthermore, when women who have gotten thin realize this grim truth, they often give up and gain back their weight. Then they think that being overweight is the source of their unhappiness, so they try to get thin again. This kind of yo-yo dieting wreaks havoc upon the body's cardiac health and organ system over time. The body is not supposed to fluctuate with gaining and losing the same twenty, sixty, or one hundred pounds over and over again.

The body also pays the price when we binge. It is very easy for frustrated women to go through phases where they decide they will be "kind" to their bodies by "giving in" and eating everything in sight, as if the body needs a gallon of Rocky Road ice cream immediately and every day. While the dieting woman tries to control the body's eating impulses, the bingeing woman succumbs to them, but the shared assumption between the two is that the body is an unruly, inferior entity that can either be controlled or given free reign. This assumption degrades the body. In describing the mindset behind compulsive bingeing, Roth explains that "we want quantity, volume, bulk. We need it—a lot of it—to go unconscious." In bingeing, women fail to appreciate food and their own bodies, and they become desensitized to the taste or nourishment of food. Roth continues, "When you like something, you pay attention to it. . . . You want to be present for every second of the rapture. Overeating does not lead to rapture. It leads to . . . being so sick that you can't think of anything but how full you are. That's not love; that's suffering."[23] To enjoy food, a woman must learn to eat in a way that feels moderate and life-giving to her body so that she becomes less hungry and eventually satisfied. Otherwise, she is creating the pain of overfullness in her body; this is a mode of self-hatred rather than self-love.

The key to resisting denigration of the body through compulsion is a learned praxis of appreciation for one's body as one's gift through this life. This idea of the body as gift, as integral to existing in the material world, has common roots in the best of Christian anthropology, particularly the Christian belief in the resurrection of the body. This doctrine suggests that final redemption includes the *entire* human person, just as the Father has raised Christ's body from the dead. And if the body

22. Ibid., 78ff.

23. Ibid., 52 and 53.

has eternal worth, then Christians have the responsibility to treat all bodies—their own flesh and the flesh of others—with love and respect.[24] Roth evokes this sense of gratitude:

> Your body is the piece of universe you've been given; as long as you have a pulse, it presents you with an ongoing shower of immediate sensate experiences. Red, salt, loneliness, heat. When a friend says something painful to you, your chest aches. When you fall in love, that same chest feels like fireworks and waterfalls and explosions of ecstasy.[25]

No matter what size you are, no matter how much cellulite or how many wrinkles you have, your body is your gift for this finite life. So anything you do for yourself needs to come from this place of fundamental self-respect rather than self-loathing.

Women are often upset by Roth's advice to love their bodies simply *because they are theirs*. When these women look in the mirror, all they see are disgusting folds and bulges, and they cannot listen to their stomachs or eat simply for physical satiety and moderate pleasure. Embodied self-hatred precludes their ability to know themselves as dignified and to know when they are actually hungry. Thus, only when they can begin to see and eventually come to marvel at the wonder, goodness, and loveliness of their own bodies can they begin to eat and move from a place of self-care rather than shame.[26] In describing her own epiphany about this, Roth writes, "eating was always about only one thing: nourishing the body. And this body wanted to live. This body loved being alive. . . . Loved being able to see, hear, touch, smell, taste—and food was a big part of how I could do that. The way I ate was another way to soar."[27] Women have to get beyond the shock of their own fleshliness, and society as a whole has to get beyond encoding fatness with disgrace. When this happens, women begin to realize that their bodies actually do not want to consume everything; physical hunger has boundaries. This realization gradually curbs the impulses for bingeing and dieting.

---

24. Karl Rahner, "The Resurrection of the Body," in his *Theological Investigations*, electronic PDF ed. (Limerick, Ireland: Mary Immaculate College, 2000) vol. 2, 203–16. Also see Rahner, "On the Theology of the Incarnation," in ibid., vol. 4, 105–20.

25. Roth, *Women, Food and God*, 122.

26. Ibid., 69.

27. Ibid., 164.

PRAXIS

It is very difficult to learn the given boundaries of one's body. It requires a gradual habituation to one's body through various concrete means over the course of one's lifetime, with varying and indeterminate degrees of success. To this end, Roth enjoins women to engage in the practice of daily meditation, first thing in the morning, in which they breathe intentionally and try to sit in stillness, aware of their bodies, especially their bellies. This practice does not remove grief or loneliness, and it can be quite frustrating, even for Roth.[28] However, meditation is key to helping one learn how to return to an awareness of her body precisely when she would rather get lost in a frenzy of unfocused desire and distraction. Meditation helps women *not* to fix themselves per se, but rather, to distinguish themselves even slightly from their pain, confusion, and loneliness and to recognize themselves as *already dignified in the stillness of their bodies*. This kind of embodied self-awareness is the opposite of compulsion and therefore gradually diminishes the impulse to eat compulsively. And this kind of meditation is entirely compatible with Christian notions of contemplative prayer in which a person recognizes herself as a locus of divine presence.[29] What is novel about Roth's approach, however, is that she connects such contemplation to women's everyday attitudes toward pasta, potato chips, and minestrone.

Roth also asks that women reconnect with their bodies by also allowing themselves to experience hunger and then learning to eat the foods that best make them feel alive and nourished. In other words, Roth is encouraging the praxis of intuitive eating, which is neither a hedonistic capitulation to ingesting massive quantities of pastry or cheese nor an act of submission to a heteronomous list of approved foods. Intuitive eating does not mean eating the "bad" food that one barely managed to avoid while dieting; it means eating foods that make the body feel alive. And to figure out what makes one's body feel alive, a person must eat calmly, when hungry, without distractions, with much pleasure, and until she is satisfied.[30] Even being able to tell when one is actually hungry is a learned ability for compulsive eaters, but Roth believes that such bodily self-knowledge is indispensable: "When you pay attention to yourself, you notice the difference between being tired and being hungry. Between being satisfied and being full. Between wanting to scream and wanting to

28. Ibid., 112–14 and 117.

29. Consult, for example, *The Interior Castle*, by sixteenth-century mystic and doctor of the Catholic Church Teresa of Ávila.

30. Roth, *Women, Food and God*, 163 and 211.

eat."[31] This kind of eating provides the best possible chance for a woman to savor her food with joy and gratitude.

Thus, when a woman does not feel hungry but experiences the impulse to eat, she must learn to allow herself to question and explore those feelings instead of numbing herself. This kind of self-questioning, in calmness, does not replace therapy (which many women struggling with compulsive eating may need), but it is a practiced mode of existing in which a woman decides that there is no sadness or anger that can kill her, and in which she allows herself to feel pain, to cry, to stare at the wall, to take a walk. To feel one's pain with this much awareness requires patience, but it is still better than refusing to sit with that pain by devouring an entire cherry cobbler. Some women who follow Roth's guidelines do lose weight as they become more aware of their real physical and spiritual desires, but such weight loss is not Roth's main point or final goal. She desires for women to love themselves, to see their own loveliness, and to use food to that end.[32] This idea freshly elucidates a Christian respect for the goodness of the embodied human creature, created and redeemed by God.

CONCLUSION

Roth's *Women, Food and God* contributes pivotal insights about the spirituality of eating and the significance of the body that resonate deeply with the best of Christian anthropology. I hope that Roth's insights not only deepen Christian anthropology, but also allow Christians to become sensitized to the misery of so many women struggling with compulsive eating and body hatred. Roth says it well when she states that "after working with so much suffering in so many women, I believe that the fact that more than half the women in this country are slogging in the quicksand of food obsession *is* a spiritual, intellectual, and political concern."[33] I hope that Roth's work will allow Christians—both women and men—to enact a sharpened political resistance to the pressures surrounding women's body image and body relation in the United States. Such political resistance may create the chance for women to opt out of body hatred and compulsive eating practices and begin the praxis of embodied self-love. In the spirit of the Word made flesh, then, may Roth's work help us care for the flesh of others and of ourselves.

31. Ibid, 194.
32. Ibid., 41 and 81.
33. Ibid., 165.

7 Purge

by B. L. GENTRY

O God, the vomit,
half-chewed nuts, pickles,
raisin skins, hash marks

of cereal. Jaw-sore,
she refolds
hands into her mouth,
praying for pleasure
rejected, offers

herself a new life,
scraped out. Images
of cellulite and dead

flood her confession.
She flushes, humped, cleansed.
Water catches in the toilet's throat.

8 Sleeping with Peaches: An Interview with Lee Price

by HEATHER SMITH STRINGER

LEE PRICE IS A figurative painter from New York who has been painting women and food for over twenty years. In her work, she addresses the intersections of food with body image, addiction, and uninhibited desire. In this interview, Price shares about her trajectory as a painter, her personal struggles with food, and the ongoing battle of women and their bodies.

The Other Journal (*TOJ*): Could you share how your career began as a figurative painter? And more specifically, how did your subject matter evolve into self-portraits and food?

Lee Price (LP): I've been painting women and food for over twenty years. In college I focused primarily on figures in environments. I would make large, life-sized paintings of women in interiors and have food randomly placed about the scene—someone holding a bunch of carrots, a stray banana on a window ledge, a seated woman feeding an orange to a dog. Back then I had no conscious understanding of what these scenes were about. It wasn't until I started this specific series, five or six years ago, that I began to have clarity about the theme. In fact, the very first painting of the series, *Full*, was very random. At that time, I was working from photographs. I had set up a scene to shoot, a sort of Alice in Wonderland thing. In the foreground, a table was set for what would seem to be a tea party and in the background a figure was sleeping in a chair. It wasn't working. I had purchased insane amounts of desserts and props for this shoot and I didn't want to waste them. So I threw an antique tablecloth down on the floor, placed all the desserts on top of it, lay down in the middle of the food, and had a friend get on a ladder and photograph it. I still didn't quite understand it, but I knew I had something that inspired me. It took a while to grasp the significance of everything.

TOJ: My sister saw a painting of yours in Seattle and could not believe that all of your work is painting and not photography. Can you tell us why figurative realism is still important in contemporary art, which perhaps seems more concerned with conceptual, abstracted, and derivative art?

LP: Yes, your sister did see a piece of mine in Seattle (*Lemon Meringue*). Tom Douglas, the owner of Cuoco restaurant, purchased it.

In regard to figurative realism, I can only say that I have always been drawn to that form of expression. I don't believe there is much of a difference between the conceptual, the abstract, and the figurative. They are different modes of communication, but in the end, you get to the same place. It seems to me that all art is about taking an idea and making it concrete. For example, I don't think it would be difficult to find three artists who are working in different modes of communication, but who are all discussing the topic of fragility and transience.

TOJ: Can you expound upon why you have chosen the nude female (mainly yourself), specific food choices and locations, the bird's eye view, and (maybe) less importantly your fairly consistent red toenail polish?

LP: These paintings are very personal. They're self-portraits, so I use myself as the model. In regard to food choices, I'm always going for something that is considered indulgent, forbidden, or comforting. The paintings are about compulsion, and excess can be an aspect of compulsive behavior. No one gets excessive with carrots.

The settings are mainly bathtubs and beds. They are private spaces, spaces of solitude, and unusual places to find someone eating. The private space emphasizes the secrecy of compulsive behavior and the unusual settings emphasize its absurdity. The solitude and peace of the setting is a good juxtaposition to the frenetic, out-of-control feel of the woman's actions.

My use of the bird's eye view gets interpreted as a voyeurism thing or a God's eye view a lot—it's neither. It's the subject looking down on herself—observing herself in the act of the compulsive behavior, being completely aware of what she is doing but unable to stop. I've spoken to friends who have had this same experience in relation to drug addiction. It's a bit like an out-of-body experience.

To be honest, the toenail polish started out as an aesthetic thing. I give a lot of thought to the color, how a particular color or image will react in a particular color scheme or setting. But really, the toenail polish has become something for my own amusement. It is commented on frequently, which makes me realize that I should be taking it a bit more seriously. I'm always thinking about the difference between "nude" and "naked." Place shoes or even a necklace on a nude model, and now the model is considered naked or sexualized. I wonder if the nail polish has the same effect.

TOJ: Your previous work around the female depicts both pleasure and self-deprecation, privacy and full disclosure, comedy and tragedy, the momentary bliss of indulgence and relaxation as well as the depression and self-loathing that usually follows. What are you uncovering or making sense of in these previous pieces?

LP: One of the things I am trying to show is how we imbue food with qualities that it does not have; we are seeking solace in an unfit source. In my earlier pieces, I feel the theme of compulsion is very evident (e.g., *Snack* and *Asleep*). Here I'm trying to convey a feeling of loss of control, a frenetic atmosphere. I'm showing how our compulsiveness distracts us from being present, how it wipes out the serenity that we would find if we could sit still. I also want to get across the absurdity of this type of behavior. We convince ourselves that the momentary reprieve that we are creating will actually last a very, very long time, that it will wipe out whatever uncomfortable feelings we're avoiding. But in reality, we're prolonging and intensifying our suffering. For most of these works, you can't see the women's faces. It is reflective of the fact that there is shame in their actions.

TOJ: As I've spent time with this series, I find it difficult to see the shame of the women in your paintings. Instead, they seem fixated on the food and the momentary ecstasy.

LP: I think many people interpret the paintings this way, that the model is having an ecstatic experience with the food. The viewer brings their own background to what they are viewing. Usually the people that see the shame are those who have experienced an eating disorder and who have felt this shame themselves.

TOJ: Your current work is similar in content to those older pieces, yet the splattering of food seems to be less of a driving force, whereas the position and gesture of the females within the paintings have become more central. What has caused the shift in your current paintings?

LP: *Sleeping with Peaches* is probably the most obvious example of the shift that you describe. It was a painting that I struggled over. I spent three months painting it and repainting it. I thought it was a colossal failure, not due to technical reasons, but because I just didn't get what it was about. It seemed vapid. It lacked the frenetic energy of my previous pieces and it seemed to lack any kind of importance. I almost gave it up. But I painstakingly finished it and grudgingly sent it off to my gallery. It wasn't until I read a critic's review that its significance became clear to me. This piece optimistically speaks about the "possibility of change" in the midst of a seemingly unending compulsion. I'm sleeping next to this food, a food that is considered nourishing as opposed to my usual junk foods, and the critic points out that I am "unconcerned enough to doze in its presence . . . the food she consumes doesn't have to be all-consuming."[1] *Sleeping with Peaches* is a transition piece, a bridge that carries me into my next series, which concentrates on the positive associations between women and food.

As I've been working on my latest pieces, two new thoughts have been popping up. First, I've been considering how we give objects of obsession/compulsion (in this case, food) qualities that we should be giving to a higher source (e.g., God or our inner voice). We see food as sacred. In *Blueberry Pancakes*, the model is seated in the tub in a posture that resembles meditation. She's holding a solitary plate of pancakes in her lap as if she is worshipping it. However, the lower third of the painting, where the model is seated, is compositionally very busy, cut-up, and frenetic in comparison to the top portion of the canvas—behind the model there is peace, but she would have to put down the pancakes and turn around to see it. My second thought, and this one was initially unintentional, is about how compulsive behavior can snuff out your life. I mean this literally, as in the case of drugs or alcohol or even food if used to an extreme degree, but I also mean that this behavior deadens you. It anesthetizes people from their actual life. In *Blueberry Pancakes*, for example, I started to see the tub as a coffin. *Ice Cream* is probably the most blatant example of this in my most current, finished works.

TOJ: How have you struggled with food in your own life? And who has helped shape your discourse around women and food?

1. Rani Molla, "Inconspicuous Consumption: *Full* Personally Masticates Our Culture's Obsession with Food," *Santa Fe Reporter*, May 4, 2001, http://www.sfreporter.com/santafe/article-6051-inconspicuous-consumption.html.

LP: Since I was very young, I struggled with issues related to food and body image. I can remember being in grade school, the thinnest and tallest girl in my class, yet trying to lose weight. A critic once commented that in my paintings "the women aren't grossly fat or pathetically thin, but their lives seem to be oppressively ruled by food."[2] And that would be a very accurate description of the role food has played in my life as I bounce between abstinence and complete loss of control. The loss of control comes when I use food to pacify myself and to fill voids other than physical hunger. I use it when I can't conceive of more appropriate avenues for filling myself. Then I experience guilt over this loss of control and fear over weight gain, so the pendulum swings back to abstinence. It's been a very, very long road to get to a less troubled place with food and I still gravitate in the direction of eating compulsively when my life is out of balance.

So much has been written in the past few decades on women and food issues. Kim Chernin's *The Hungry Self* and Susie Orbach's *Fat Is a Feminist Issue*,[3] which are both books that I read more than twenty years ago, were probably the most influential books in regard to my understanding of the psychology of eating disorders and, more specifically, compulsive eating.

TOJ: How has American culture influenced your trajectory as a female painter who engages, primarily, with your body?

LP: I grew up in a household of women. I lived with my mother and two older sisters. My father, for the most part, was absent from my childhood. Both of my grandfathers had passed away before I was born. I had no male relatives nearby. This obviously has affected how I see and react to my environment.

In terms of the influence of American culture, I believe that our culture objectifies women and encourages women to objectify themselves. So I have a great concern over my works being interpreted in a sexualized way. I also believe that we

2. Greg Stacy, "Eoin Breadon and Jason Chakravarty Haunt @Space Gallery," *OC Weekly*, May 1, 2008, http://www.ocweekly.com/2008-05-01/culture/certain-doom/.

3. Kim Chernin, *The Hungry Self: Women, Eating and Identity* (New York: Times Books, 1985); Susie Orbach, *Fat Is a Feminist Issue: The Anti-Diet Guide to Permanent Weight Loss* (New York: Berkley, 1978).

are all sexual beings and to negate that aspect would be dishonest. Therefore, I'm constantly going back and forth between my concerns that my works are either too far in the territory of "cheesecake" or that I have completely eradicated the model's sexuality. When I'm choosing poses, I often find myself leaning toward images that repulse instead of attract. However, I still need to bring the viewer in. Get them to want to look. Optimally I look for images that initially attract and then, after some scrutiny, disturb.

TOJ: The perspective you paint from is somewhat nostalgic of pre-Manet figurative painting (e.g., Manet's *Olympia*), in which the female never held the gaze of the viewer, rather the viewer was able to look and objectify without much anxiety of being caught or confronted. And this created a significant power differential. Often these nude females display some degree of awareness that they are being observed, whether it is from modeling for the male artist or the foreknowledge that the finished painting will be looked at many times over. But your nude females seem to not know of their audience gazing downward at them. How does this kind of awareness or lack of awareness relate to your paintings?

LP: In a few of my paintings, the figure is *eyeing* the viewer. In these paintings, the figure's actions are uncensored and an absence of guilt is much more prevalent. These are meant to convey an acceptance of hunger, a lack of guilt about having an appetite—not just with food, but in general.

However, in most of my paintings, the model is watching herself. She is utterly consumed in her actions. She has no awareness of being seen, and the private environments in which her actions are taking place remove any concern for being caught. When I'm choosing poses, I try to be very conscious of conveying a feeling of "How would I behave if I knew no one could see me?" So the viewer is simply watching the model watch herself. It is reflective of the effect that compulsive behavior has in reality. It creates a wall in which others may see you but no true communication or interaction is taking place. And I hope that my paintings are thus opening up true communication and interactions, that they are making hunger and compulsive consumption and the shame and secrecy with which we resort to around these matters a public discussion.

Lee Price, *Full*, 2007, oil on linen, 44 x 54 in. Courtesy of private collector.

Lee Price, *Lemon Meringue*, 2010, oil on linen, 32 x 72 in. Courtesy of private collector.

Lee Price, *Snack*, 2008, oil on linen, 52 x 40 in. Courtesy of private collector.

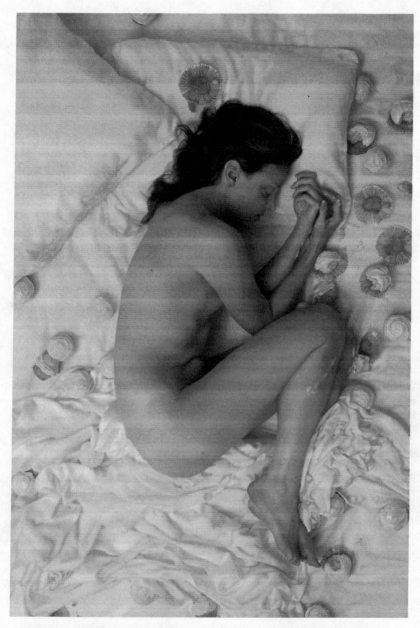

Lee Price, *Asleep*, 2007, oil on linen, 56 x 38 in. Courtesy of private collector.

LEFT: Lee Price, *Blueberry Pancakes*, 2011, oil on linen, 60 x 28 in. Courtesy of private collector.

BELOW: Lee Price, *Ice Cream*, 2011, oil on linen, 31 x 62 in. Courtesy of Evoke Contemporary Gallery.

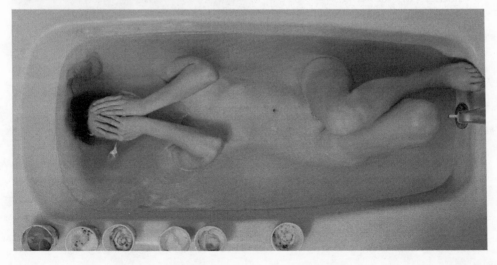

9 Portions

by KATHERINE LO

Home from the grocery store,
I clear out the old food
to make way for the new—
the container of eight or nine cherry
tomatoes shriveled to dull red prunes,
the partial package of shredded cheese
sporting a fuzzy beard of mold,
the half loaf of bread stale-hardened and dry,
the clump of lettuce leaves blackened and limp—
a spoiled feast filling me with guilt at this reminder
of waste when so many are hungry, but also sadness
at how food is portioned for those who eat
with others, not alone.

10 Feeding Bodies and the Theology of Taking Lives: An Interview with Norman Wirzba

by JON TSCHANZ

ACCORDING TO THE GOSPEL of John, when Jesus first appears after his resurrection he is mistaken for a gardener. He comes to Mary Magdalene, who is weeping at the empty tomb, and she asks him what has been done with Jesus's body. But perhaps this case of mistaken identity tells us something about the character of God. In a culture that relies on fast, convenient, and cheap food, perhaps it is time to reclaim Jesus as the gardener, the one who gives life and is the source of life, and perhaps it is time to allow that understanding to change how we view our relationship between faith and food. Norman Wirzba in his newest book, *Food and Faith: A Theology of Eating* (Cambridge University Press, 2011), has pointed to the endless and essential connections between food and faith that Christians everywhere need to hear. In this interview, Wirzba leads us to a renewed understanding of food and faith, giving us a hope to imagine something new, something Jesus has in store for us—a foretaste of heaven, right here.

The Other Journal (TOJ): In your new book, *Food and Faith: A Theology of Eating*, you explore what food means in the life of faith. Why should what we put in our mouths matter?

Norman Wirzba (NW): There's a lot to think about there. On the one hand, we have to pay attention to who we are as Christians. My worry is that for so much of Christian history, and especially in America today, a lot of Christians think about themselves primarily as individual souls. The fact that they are bodies doesn't really seem to matter much. Eating is a great way to talk about human embodiment. It's also a great way to talk about human embodiment in its relationship to lots of other bodies, and ultimately in its relationship to God as the one who nurtures the whole of creation so that we can have life.

In my book food became this wonderful way for me to open up a whole set of questions that aren't on the table for a lot of Christians, questions about what it means to be one of God's creatures living in the world today in a way that will be more responsible. We know that a lot of the eating that we do is bad for us physically, socially, and spiritually, but it's also bad for creation. Eating is one of those great and complex kinds of activities that opens out into the whole realm of human existence in its relationship to other humans, in its relationship to other creatures, and then in its relationship to God.

When I first started working on the book, I had friends that would say, "Why are you writing a book on food? Christians aren't supposed to worry about food, right? It's in the Gospels. Jesus says in Matthew that we're not to worry about what we're going to eat or what we're going to wear." But the truth is that whenever we eat, we're making a statement about who we think we are and how we value the world. What would it mean to see eating as receiving God's creation? Eating is not just a physiological act. I think it's an ecological act and a profoundly spiritual act.

TOJ: How do eating and the act of saying grace show our place in the world?

NW: I think we could start with how our eating shows us to be *interdependent* creatures. We've sort of gotten used to the idea—and there's a lot in our culture that encourages us to think this way—that we are self-standing beings. And if not self-standing beings, we are at least self-legislating beings, which means we get to decide for ourselves the kind of life we want, and we want to have that life on our own terms. We love the kinds of conveniences and technologies that allow us to have life cheaply, conveniently, and on demand. And what that does is it gives us a really distorted sense of who we are, because we then start to think that the world exists for us. That's a profoundly damaging view of the world because the world doesn't exist for us; the world exists for God. And so the question should be, how can our eating show that we understand this? And when you think about how we live and what Eric Schlosser called the "Fast Food Nation,"[1] we see that eating has become primarily an economic act where everything hinges upon cheapness, speed, and efficiency, and in doing that, we're doing great harm to our bodies, to agricultural workers, and

1. See Eric Schlosser, *Fast Food Nation: The Dark Side of the All-American Meal* (Boston: Houghton Mifflin, 2001).

to animals. We're destroying our fields. To have all these cheap, convenient foods means that we're not adequately caring for things.

Our duty to care for things is, I think, fundamental. It starts in Genesis, where we have a kind of foundational story in which God says we're supposed to take care of the garden. Through much of our eating today we're not taking care of the garden. When you look beyond the physical act of consumption and start to ask questions about the stories behind the food—what's really going on to get that food to us?— I think you get a picture showing us that our eating and our living are not right. Ultimately, I want to help us understand what it means to be a responsible, faithful creature in the world. Eating can be a powerful way to do that.

You also ask about saying grace, which I think is really important. I grew up saying grace, and I imagine lots of people have. The act of saying grace can become formulaic, but it can also have a lot of value. We're all very busy people and that means we don't reflect on what we're doing much of the time. We just go through our day by rote, and because we haven't stopped to think about what we're doing, we continue in ways that are damaging to creation and to ourselves. So an important part of saying grace is stopping and clearing our minds of the clutter, worry, and anxiety of all that's going on in our heads. Then we turn our attention to what's on the table. What we discover is that we've got a history of living and dying happening on that table. We've got a history of agricultural workers and cooks and people who have produced and prepared the food. We need time to take that in because, otherwise, we are more likely to abuse what we take for granted, what we don't value. My hope is that we will learn to value food, not make an idol of it, but value it as God's gift given to us.

And how do we learn to receive the gift gratefully? That leads into the next dimension of saying grace, where we learn to try to be thankful for what our life depends upon. To be grateful will invariably put us into a position of humility because we understand that without the gifts of family and friends who nurture us along the way, and without God's gifts of fields and water and plants and animals and bees, we'd be done! Without worms and bees, there's no fertility or pollination; and without fertility and pollination, we don't eat; and without eating, we don't live. And so I think eating can be a powerful sort of lens to get us into a deeper understanding of who we are and where we are and on who and what we're dependent.

TOJ: You mentioned being at the table, and so I'm wondering what your thoughts are on what it means for us to sit at the table, especially in acts of hospitality and justice and mission as we participate in God's reconciliation of the world?

NW: We're pretty unusual today in that we have so many people eating individually and on the run. There was a famous book awhile back called *Bowling Alone*.[2] You could get at many of these same kinds of issues by writing a book called *Eating Alone*. I think this way of eating promotes a very distorted view about who we are as people and also about what food is.

One way to describe food is as God's way of saying to us, "I love you. I want to nurture you into life." When we understand food in this very theological sort of way, that in eating we are the beneficiaries of God's love, the only appropriate response is to turn our life into a source of nurture for others. That means coming to understand that eating is not primarily about consumption but about sharing life with others so that together we can realize our full potential. When we discover that there are people in the world who don't have enough to eat or who eat in ways that are unhealthy to them in the long term or who live in food deserts like you find in many inner cities where they don't have access to good food, I think the church must become serious about feeding these people. When you look at the Gospels, Jesus is doing lots of things with bodies—touching them and healing them, for instance—but he is also feeding them. And if we are supposed to be witnesses to this Christ, I think it would be really fantastic if churches were to say, "We're in the feeding business, *literally*, and that means that we're going to try to make our church a physical place in which even the growing of food, and then also the sharing of food, happens regularly, a place where people understand that we're not just interested in individual souls."

Jesus cared about souls, but he always understood persons as *embodied* creatures who need physical touch, physical healing, and physical feeding. And I don't think the church should be any different. It should understand that its mission has to reach out to the bodies of other human beings, which means, then, that you have to worry about all the bodies those human beings come into contact with—the bodies of animals, the bodies of plants, the bodies of fields and forests, and all the rest.

TOJ: And Jesus spends a lot of his time eating with people, right?

2. Robert D. Putnam, *Bowling Alone: The Collapse and Revival of American Community* (New York: Simon and Schuster, 2000).

NW: Oh, yeah. When I first started working on the book, I was amazed at how much food shows up in the Bible. It's all over the place. We don't pay attention to that or think that it's of any great significance because, for the most part, we live in a culture that doesn't ascribe a lot of significance to food. I know that there are things like the Food Network now on cable TV, but it's a spectator sport. Many of these cooking shows are not meant to instruct you in your own cooking or in your own growing of food. In fact, a lot of the commercials for these kinds of shows are about convenience foods that you pop in your microwave. These shows are about pyrotechnics, about selling kitchen equipment, but they're not about making us better eaters, better producers of food, better sharers of food.

TOJ: What happens when we no longer see food as gift, when we begin to understand food as this commodity, as this product to be purchased? And how does that kind of imagination shape the way we think about food when it becomes just a product?

NW: People don't appreciate how industrial food production signals a new phase in human history. For generations, millennia even, we've understood that eating is an ecological and agricultural act, which meant that our eating was always bound to ecological limits and ecological potential—a person can't abuse the land for long and expect to be able to eat from it. But what's happened in agribusiness is that we no longer understand eating as an ecological reality; we understand it as an economic reality. That means that when we decide how we grow food, we are not asking about the fertility of the soil, the supply of water, or the consequences of poison. From an ecological standpoint, we have to protect soil fertility and water purity, because when you lose those, you lose everything! But an economic way of thinking about agriculture is primarily concerned about price; it's primarily concerned about efficiencies. And as soon as you go down that path, you may compromise soil fertility, use up or poison your waters, abuse your animals, and abuse your agricultural workers because you're doing it all for the noble aim of the cheapest price! For a lot of people, all that matters is that the food is available and that it is really, really cheap.

Cheap food, however, conceals a lot of costs to human and ecological health. As ecological systems and agricultural communities and workers suffer more and more, we're going to find ourselves in a position where the food system itself will be completely unsustainable and will collapse. I don't know exactly how that's going to look. Agribusiness depends entirely on cheap oil. As the cost of fossil fuels continues to rise, we may have multiple food crises. In North America we don't spend that much of our income on food, but many people live in parts of the world where a daily income of two dollars a day is normal, and these people don't have margins to work with. As the price of oil rises, food riots develop around the world because the very staples they need, be it rice or bread or some other cheap food, have been priced out of range and so they can't eat. When you have people who can't eat, what have you got? You have a context for tremendous political unrest, let alone all the misery that accompanies starvation.

TOJ: We do see some places where people are starting to think about these things, but some people would say that it's very "bourgeois." How we can move toward something different, especially an alternative that might work in places like the inner city, where people don't have the funds to be a part of that kind of culture and don't have access to certain kinds of foods because of where they're located?

NW: That's a really important question because there is a kind of elitism that you can see in foodie culture, if I can put it that way. There's even idolatry going on here. The *Atlantic* magazine ran a March 2011 article by B. R. Myers that illustrates how a lot of our food writers today are guilty of gluttony. The use of the language of the seven deadly sins by a secular writer like Myers is pretty insightful. I don't know that I accept all the aspects of his critique, but he's right to say that eating can become an aspect of highbrow culture in which all that we care about is the exotic quality of the food. Quality often means a higher price, which then takes the nutritious food out of the reach of poor people who could never afford to buy it. You don't find poor folks hanging out at Whole Foods. So, yes, there's an important dimension to that charge of elitism in some of the food movement.

I think there are lots of ways to respond to it. I think we have to understand how government policy right now subsidizes the production of really bad, unhealthy food. It's hard to call some of it food because it's so highly processed that it's not anything that comes out of the ground. That's a policy decision not an ecological decision. Why couldn't we then say that we're going to start supporting the production of healthy food so that the subsidies that now make high fructose corn syrup so cheap—and which shows up in everything—are instead going to be used to support people who are growing real food and organically grown fruits and vegetables, and humanely raised beef, poultry, and dairy?

We need to get out of the habit of thinking that as eaters we are only food consumers, that the only relationship we have with food is a purchasing relationship. Historically, almost everybody was involved in the growing of the food they ate.

They didn't grow everything, certainly, but they grew a lot of it. And for the things they didn't grow, they had personal relationships with the people who did. And so you understood that you had to be involved in the growing of food. I'd like to advocate that people start growing some of their own food. You don't need a lot of land to do it. If you've only got a small apartment, start by having a couple of pots where you can grow something. That would be really important.

In urban areas, including those inner-city food deserts that I mentioned, there is land that's not being used for anything. Some of it is municipal land; some of it has been abandoned. There's no reason why that land can't be taken over by community groups and individuals who say, "Let's start growing some food here!" Why can't churches be partnering with community groups to start growing good, nutritious food? A lot of the price that's associated with food these days is related to the labor, technology, packaging, and distance it's traveled, so when you grow your own food, you can wipe out all those costs and get it a lot cheaper.

Another aspect of this is that churches are sitting on a lot of land, a lot of manicured lawns, bushes, and pavement. Why can't some of that land be turned into gardens that then produce food so that the people who can't afford to buy good food can work with community or church members to produce healthy food? In parts of the world where for six or seven months you can't be growing things outside, people can also recover the art of preserving food—they can learn to can tomatoes, make salsa, or whatever. That doesn't mean we have to do everything—that's a big job— but we can do something. And that can take a lot of pressure off of people who right now are looking at food they can't afford but would love to eat. I think that's a really important issue for the church to take up.

TOJ: Some of the things you've talked about are similar to what other popular culture figures have talked about. Michael Pollan, for example, has made some of the same moves, but you're trying to understand food theologically. I'm wondering what the gospel has to say here. What do the life, death, and resurrection of Jesus have to say here? And how is that different from the movement of mainstream culture? Or how do Jesus's life, death, and resurrection influence how you view things?

NW: At the end of *The Omnivore's Dilemma*, Pollan has this party scene where he, along with his friends, puts together a meal where everything has been either hunted or gathered. They've spent a lot of time preparing this big feast, and as they're sitting around the table, he says that he was longing for a language that wasn't at his disposal. It was the kind of language that he would call a religious sort of language, the sacred. And I think Pollan's right in suggesting that this is the direction that you have to go if you're going to talk about food in its real depth. I respect and have learned a lot from Pollan—I think he's got a lot of very important things to teach us—but I think you have to go further, you have to go in the direction of theology, because you have to be able to deal with the fact that eating is a matter of life and death.[3]

When we eat, even if we're vegetarians, we are taking the lives of others. And the question is, how do you make yourself worthy of the life of another that you now consume? And that's a very, very difficult question. It gets us to the heart of what it means to be a creature, because God creates a world in which everything that is alive eats, but for anything to eat, another must die. And this is where I think theology has so much to offer, because when you look at the Old Testament and the New Testament, you find that there is this use of the language of sacrifice. There are plenty of people who would want to say it's time to put sacrifice outside of our theological imaginations, but I think that that's precisely the wrong way to go. A lot of suspicion about sacrifice rests upon a misunderstanding of what it is. We look at the sacrifice and we fixate on the altar and the slaughter of the animal. We don't pay nearly enough attention to the giving of the person to that animal in its nurture, in its protection, in its rearing so that the animal could be presented to God. Historically speaking, the case can be made that the offering of the animal was always accompanied by the self-offering of the person making the sacrifice. It was the same with the grains that were offered at the temple.

When you live in an agricultural society, to offer the first fruits of your fields and to offer the healthy animal in your flock is to make a profound commitment of yourself to God. Jesus shows us this in his ministry in an ultimate and practical way because he shows us that to live the Christian life is to give yourself away. You give yourself away not by despising yourself. You give yourself away by devoting your life to the nurture of others, even the nurture of the whole of creation because without the creation, none of us can live. Theologically speaking, I think what Jesus shows us is that if you want to be a truly Christian eater, you have to learn to eat in such a way that you aren't simply taking things from the world, but that you're also giving yourself to the world in its care, in its protection. I think that's really what the Eucharist is all about.

The Eucharist is about eating Jesus, drinking Jesus, so that he can enter into us, and being now inside of us, he can redirect all of our activities so that we can

---

3. See Michael Pollan, *The Omnivore's Dilemma: A Natural History of Four Meals* (New York: Penguin, 2006).

talk about a christological form of raising animals, raising plants, and pursuing an agricultural economy. Once we have Christ in us, Christ transforms our vision, and transforms our expectations about what's important, what should be valued, what needs to be cared for, what needs to be protected. Because of Christ, all of these things now appear to us in a new light. I think that's the really profound thing the Scriptures show us, that there is this uniquely self-sacrificial way of relating to food and the world that then makes genuine sharing possible.

TOJ: So Jesus helps transform our imaginations, so to speak. He gives us a new way to look at food, in a sense, so everything kind of goes through Jesus.

NW: It's like when you come to the Eucharist table, and you see that the bread is not just bread, that the wine or grape juice is not just wine and grape juice. It's the life of the world. And the Eucharist table extends to our kitchen tables because we don't just do this as a little memorial that we tuck away and sequester from the rest of our lives. We eat Jesus so that we can be nurtured into the life that we are supposed to live every day, which means that our dining room table now should be informed by the Eucharist table.

TOJ: You have said that as we grow up, food plays a big role in our church life. And we see this, for example, in Sunday potlucks. Why is it, though, that we fail to see the connection between food and the gospel? How can we be faithful eaters?

NW: We are so gnostic, even when we're trying not to be. We really think that Christianity is about saving souls and getting our souls to heaven. Church members get together to eat all this unhealthy food that has been destructive to the land and abusive of animals and agricultural workers, and we do this because we really don't think our bodies matter. This is, of course, in direct violation of what the gospel teaches—that Jesus becomes incarnate, in the flesh, and is seeking the reconciliation of all bodies in creation. And so, because we have become so gnostic in the way we think about the world, there can be a disconnection between our lives and the message of the good news, which Colossians 1:23 says has been preached to *all* creatures. This biblical directive should change dramatically the way we relate to each other in bodily form.

You might also say that we're captive to the culture and thus eat the same way everybody else does. I'm not in a position to judge how everybody else eats because I'm not a perfect eater myself, so I must be careful here and can't go around pointing the finger. However, I think that as we read scripture together and reflect on what eating looks like when understood in a scriptural way, we're going to start changing some of the things we do when we have a church potluck. Maybe we will second-guess using the cheapest meats and vegetables and will be willing to purchase meats and vegetables that were raised responsibly. Maybe we'll think about whether we're serving our food on Styrofoam or disposable products that are not compostable. Maybe we will start asking questions about who is doing the cooking—is it assumed that the women do all the cooking and cleanup and that the men just sit around and eat, or is this a shared kind of work? Once we bring a eucharistic or christological imagination to this very basic, simply wonderful action of eating together as a church, you just never know what's going to be the result, what kinds of good things can happen from that. I happen to think that if churches ate together more frequently that would be tremendous because so much good ministry can happen when people are around a table, eating together, sharing their life. I don't think we should ever underestimate the importance of that. Yet we must make sure that act of eating together is a faithful witness to the kind of eating Christ wants us to do.

TOJ: My church recently read a passage out of John that seems relevant here—I am wondering, how do we understand Jesus as Gardener? What does it mean that outside the tomb, in this place of death, Mary Magdalene mistakes Jesus for the gardener, as the one who brings life?

NW: That's a great question and it's really hard to know exactly what to make of this reference in John where Jesus is mistaken for a gardener. I take it back to Genesis where the first description you really have of God is as a gardener. In Genesis chapter 2, it says God planted a garden in Eden to the east, and that ought to stop us dead in our tracks because we're not used to thinking about God in that way. I have never heard a sermon about God the gardener. And that's striking because this is one of the first passages in the Bible where we're introduced to who God is, and I think it's significant that God is not initially portrayed as the warrior but as the gardener. You can trace this language of God gardening throughout the Old Testament. It shows up in many of the psalms; it shows up in the prophetic literature. I think you can understand this language of God as the primordial gardener in that God is constantly nurturing all of life, protecting life, making sure that it has what it needs to survive and to flourish. God gives to the world its fertility! I think maybe what's so instructive about John's gospel is that the garden is the site of resurrection and new life. Perhaps the resurrection life that Christ makes possible in us now has to have these ecological dimensions, these gardening dimensions, and perhaps, having seen how

Christ overcomes death, we can now approach the death of the world differently and gardening in it differently. That might be one way to go about it, but that's a fair bit of conjecture.

TOJ: I'd like to end with the first question that you asked in the first class that I ever took with you; you started off the class by asking this question. Will there be eating in heaven?

NW: I think there will be eating in heaven. Of course, I can't say that with any kind of certainty or serious confidence. Throughout the church's history, others have explored this question and answered no. For instance, Tertullian says that we're not going to eat in heaven because God is the one who provides for all of our needs, and in heaven we are participating in the life of God, so there is no more need. That makes perfect sense. But is eating only about the satisfaction of need? I don't think it is. I think eating is fundamentally about establishing a life of communion. There are all sorts of ways to talk about what that communion looks like—how does the Trinity, for instance, help us understand what that communion looks like? But certainly communion is about learning to share in the life of each other, and eating is one of the most primordial ways we have for sharing in the life of each other.

Since, as Christians, we don't believe in the immortality of the soul but the resurrection of bodies, I think it's significant and quite possible that in heaven we will continue to eat. What its precise character will be, of course, I have no idea. One of the reasons it will be a transformed eating is that right now, for me to eat, another must die. Will that be the character of the eating in heaven? I don't think so. But what other kind of eating could there be? There's a wonderful hint of this, I think, in the story of Moses. When Moses is out in the wilderness before he agrees to lead the people of Israel, God encounters Moses in a burning bush. The remarkable thing about that burning bush is that it is not consumed. In fact, its presence is sort of magnified, heightened in the very burning of it. I wonder whether, since eating is a kind of burning—digestion is a kind of burning—it may be possible that the eating we do in heaven will be like a burning that doesn't consume but instead magnifies to fuller vision and clarity what is there. I certainly don't know, but I think we need to use our imaginations here. I think there are scriptural and theological grounds for saying that eating would occur in heaven because it's such a wonderful way of participating in life with each other. And it just tastes so good!

TOJ: That's great. Do you have any final words or thoughts?

NW: Just to be merciful with each other. It's very easy to become judgmental when we start thinking about eating and not realize or appreciate how intensely personal eating is. People eat the way they do, not always because of choice or even because of some conscious decision—it's just what they do. For us to become better eaters it's going to take a lot of time and a lot of mercy. So I try to tell people, "Let's work on that." If we start there, we've made a good beginning.

11 Bread, Surpassing the Savour of a Fair White Loaf to One Who Is Starving: Food and the Culture of Hobbits

by MATTHEW DICKERSON

FOR WRITERS LIKE MYSELF who have spent decades studying, teaching, and writing about the works of the late J. R. R. Tolkien, one of the advantages of the success of Peter Jackson's film adaptations is that many magazines (like this one) are interested in publishing articles about Tolkien. One of the disadvantages is that many people today know Tolkien's works only by the films. Those who have only seen Jackson's films or have given the books only a cursory reading may think of Tolkien's writings primarily in terms of great, epic (and cinematic) battles. What may be surprising to those who have not read the books closely is that the narrator seems far less interested in describing these battles than in describing Middle-earth itself, and its cultures and people. Indeed, the narrator is particularly fond of describing the food and the various traditions and practices surrounding meals and eating in Middle-earth.

Consider for a moment some of the memorable meals shared by hobbits in *The Hobbit* and *The Lord of the Rings*. And consider the surprising detail with which the fare is described. Both stories begin with famous feasts—"parties" they are called—one unexpected and one long expected. At his "Unexpected Party" in the first chapter of *The Hobbit*, Bilbo finds himself feeding thirteen dwarves and one wizard. The fare includes seedcake and other cakes, raspberry jam, apple tart, mince pies, cheese, pork pie, salad, eggs, and biscuits. The beverages include tea, coffee, beer, ale, porter, and wine. The scene is festive. Before those gathered get down to the official business of the evening—planning a journey to Lonely Mountain so that the dwarves can reclaim their long-lost treasure from the dragon Smaug—there is a considerable amount of music and storytelling, as well as the enjoyment of good food.

The second chapter of *The Hobbit* also gets its name from a meal, "Roast Mutton"—though in this case, the referenced meal is being consumed by three trolls who would also like to feast on some fresh hobbit and dwarf. In subsequent chapters, Bilbo and the company of dwarves enjoy the hospitality of the wise elven figure Elrond in Rivendell (ch. 3), and then later, a very memorable meal of "rabbits, hares, and a small sheep" eaten with the eagles high up in their eyrie (ch. 6). They enjoy several vegetarian meals of bread, butter, honey, nuts, dried fruits, and mead with the powerful Norse were-bear character Beorn—meals "such as they had not had since they left . . . Elrond" (ch. 7).

The party at the beginning of *The Fellowship of the Ring*, the first volume of *The Lord of the Rings*, is even more elaborate than the one at the beginning of *The Hobbit*, with at least 144 guests and many weeks of preparation. Tolkien devotes a significant part of a chapter to describing the foods and beverages consumed, who is there to share them, and what transpires at the party. Then, as Frodo, Sam, Merry, and Pippin leave the Shire and make their way across Middle-earth, the story seems to move—like life itself—from meal to meal, with many of the most important scenes taking place around shared food. Frodo, Sam, and Pippin are only one full day away from Bag End on their journey, and still well within the Shire, when they encounter Gildor and his company of elves. The hobbits end up joining the elves for a meal, and once again—despite the pressing matter of the hobbits' recent encounter with the frightful Black Rider and the many questions that remain unanswered, all of which are critical to the tale—the narrator takes the time to describe in some detail both the setting and the fare. The meal provided by the elves includes "bread, surpassing the savour of a fair white loaf to one who is starving; and fruit sweet as wildberries and richer than the tended fruits of gardens." The beverage is a "fragrant draught, cool as a clear fountain, golden as a summer afternoon." Despite all the adventures he will later be a part of, this meal is after remembered by Sam as one of the "chief events" of his life (ch. 3).

After this, but while the hobbits are still within the Shire, comes a meal with Farmer Maggot and his family, a more homey hobbit fare than the meal provided by the elves: "beer in plenty, and a mighty dish of mushrooms and bacon, besides much other solid farmhouse fare" (ch. 4). And before dining at Crickhollow with their friend Fredegar "Fatty," the hobbits *thought* and *talked* about a drink (and presumably a meal) from the Golden Perch. Soon after leaving the Shire, there are several meals in the house of Tom Bombadil with Tom and his wife Goldberry. Two of these are mentioned specifically. The hobbits are fed, for their first supper, "yellow cream and honeycomb, and white bread, and butter; milk, cheese, and green herbs and ripe berries gathered." Then, for breakfast the next morning, the hobbits must have had another excellent meal, for they "left the table late and only when it was beginning to look rather empty" (ch. 7).

After a near-disaster at the Barrow Downs, the hobbits have yet another meal with Bombadil, which helps them recover their strength. Not too long after this, they have a meal at the Prancing Pony, and once again we are told explicitly what the fare was: "hot soup, cold meats, a blackberry tart, new loaves, slabs of butter, and half a ripe cheese: good plain food, as good as the Shire could show, and homelike enough to dispel the last of Sam's misgivings (already much relieved by the excellence of the beer)" (ch. 9). And this brings us only to the end of the first part of six in *The Lord of the Rings*!

In all this time, all of these meals, each described lovingly and with considerable detail, there is only one battle: the fight at Weathertop. Contrary to the impression one might get from Peter Jackson's film adaptation, this is not merely a great action-adventure full of battles and swords and sorcery. This lack of balance—food everywhere and hardly a battle to be seen—may come as a surprise. How does Tolkien get away with this? How does he keep his readers attention given that he spends more time describing food and meals than he does battles? And *why* does he take this approach?

There are many possible answers to the last of these questions, and likely some truth to many of these answers, but the simple and obvious one may be the most important: Tolkien devotes so much attention to his vivid descriptions of food and meals and the cultures surrounding them, to *what* we eat and *how* we eat and how we eat *together*, because he believed that these are the things that really matter in life. Our approach to food really is important. It makes a difference in our lives. And while the adventure of the stories catches our attention, it is these seemingly more mundane aspects of the daily lives of hobbits and the other people of Middle-earth that make us understand the characters and care about them, and ultimately, therefore, care what happens in the great wars. Put another way, it is the importance of what happens around these meals that makes the sacrifice of war worthwhile and that lets the reader know there is something worth fighting about. These things are what make the story matter to Tolkien as a writer and to us as readers.

Which brings us back to the story and to the action of danger and battles—the danger grows after the four hobbits depart from Elrond's safe haven at Rivendell, and from that point on we have more battles, both large and small. Admittedly, the balance of description shifts somewhat away from food and meals and toward danger as the hobbits get farther from their homes in the Shire. Yet at Rivendell and afterward, the four hobbits again have meals that are described with more detail than might be seen as necessary to the story—detail that often surpasses the level of detail used to describe the battles. Among the more significant meals and feasts, we could list the fellowship's parting meal with the elf Galadriel (it is called a "feast," although the fare is not described) near the end of book 2; the numerous meals that Merry and Pippin have at the house of the giant Ent, or tree shepherd, Treebeard, in book 3, chapter 4 (the Ent draught brought "refreshment" and "vigor" and left their hair standing on end); the reunion meal that Merry and Pippin share with Aragorn, Legolas, and Gimli in Isengard (bread, wine, beer, salted pork, and rashers of bacon) at the end of book 3; the meal cooked by Sam in the pots and pans he had carried all the way from the Shire in book 4 (in a chapter named after that meal: "Herbs and Stewed Rabbit"); the dinner Frodo and Sam eat with Faramir in Ithilien (not only do the hobbits appreciate the "pale yellow wine, cool and fragrant," as well as the bread and batter, salted meats, dried fruits, and good red cheese, but they also appreciate the chance to eat a meal with "clean hands and clean knives and plates"), described in book 4, chapter 5; and in book 5, Pippin's meal with Denethor in chapter 1, along with Merry's meal with King Théoden in Rohan in chapter 3.

To say, then, that food and meals play an important role in Tolkien's Middle-earth writings would be an understatement. Of course, it is apparent to even the most casual reader of *The Hobbit* and *The Lord of the Rings* that food is important to hobbits. We all remember that hobbits are fond of six meals a day, including two dinners, if they can get it. As the prologue to *The Lord of the Rings* points out, they "eat, and drink, often and heartily." Indeed, "growing food and eating it occupied most of their time." Indeed, so obviously important are food and eating to hobbits that, beyond an occasional casual reference to their passion for food, few scholars and critics bother to carefully explore the importance of food in Tolkien's narratives (though some certainly have done a good job with this). It is debatable whether food is *more* important to the narrative than fighting—despite the previously mentioned predominance, at least in book 1, of meal scenes over battle scenes—but the idea that it *might* be more important is certainly not as farfetched as it might seem to those who think only of the typical writing in the genre of heroic fantasy. The fact that food is anywhere near as prevalent as war and battle in Tolkien's narrative is itself noteworthy.

But what *is* the importance of meals? Among hobbits especially—though it can also be seen among elves, men, Ents, and even at times dwarves—eating is a *communal* act: food and eating connect hobbits with each other, with strangers they encounter, and with the earth itself. And in many ways, the hobbit culture of the Shire, and especially the hobbits' approach to eating, is presented by Tolkien as a model of healthy society. The Shire, and the ways and lives of hobbits, is something that the wise of Middle-earth, including the future king Aragorn and the wise wizard Gandalf, and later Frodo himself, believe is worth great sacrifice in order to save.

Regarding the role of shared meals as a means toward peace, it is important to note that the people of the Shire are fond of eating together, and there are no wars within the Shire. The prologue explicitly links these points in noting that hobbits are "slow to quarrel," that they do not kill anything for sport, and that "growing food and eating it occupied most of their time." Tolkien also illustrates the value of the communal sharing of food in extended family meal scenes, such as in the homes of the Maggot and Cotton farming families near the start and end of *The Lord of the Rings*, respectively, as well as in the much larger communal feasts, like Bilbo's birthday party, and in the popularity of inns and taverns in the Shire. The close bond that exists and continues to develop between Frodo, Sam, Merry, and Pippin almost certainly owes a great debt to time spent together over food and drink. As noted, Tolkien's narrative does not skimp in describing several of these scenes.

But the importance of meals to community does not pertain only to hobbits within the Shire. We also see that eating meals together helps join the lives of hobbits with the lives of strangers, and even with those for whom hobbits would have a natural distrust (which, as we learn, includes almost everybody outside their own little corners of the Shire). The most poignant example in *The Hobbit* may be the vegetarian meal served by the were-bear Beorn to Bilbo and his fellow travelers. Before the meal, Beorn is as distrustful of strangers as are hobbits, whereas after the meal the hobbit and his company of dwarves feel they have found a friend. In *The Lord of the Rings*, the narrative is full of these examples, and a closer look at these examples is illuminating. A long period of fear and distrust between Frodo and Farmer Maggot is broken by a wonderful meal together, where one hobbit, Farmer Maggot—though he has reason to be fearful of the general situation, having just encountered a Black Rider, and he also has reason to distrust Frodo based on the young Baggins's old habit of stealing mushrooms—makes a choice to show hospitality in the form of a shared meal. Frodo's response to the farmer and his hospitality, though spoken before the meal was actually served, tells the tale: "I've been in terror of you and your dogs for over thirty years, Farmer Maggot, though you may laugh to hear it. It's a pity: for I've missed a good friend" (bk. 1, ch. 4).

Several examples of meals I have mentioned previously also show a joining of lives, even among diverse strangers. That is to say, they show how somewhat reclusive and provincial hobbits find their lives joined to those in the world outside the Shire, even members of other races: the elves in Gildor's company, elves of Rivendell and Lothlórien, Fangorn and the Ents, and Faramir and the men of Gondor. In the latter two cases especially, the meeting of two hobbits with these strangers begins with fear and distrust on both parts. And in both cases a meal is shared among strangers, and the distrust begins to fade. By the end, close bonds of friendship have been forged.

Hobbits, perhaps because of their practice of eating locally, growing their own food, and consuming it together, are also tied to their land. When Frodo sets off on his quest, he is explicit in stating that he not only wants to save his fellow hobbits, but the Shire itself. When they return, Sam (as new mayor) devotes time not only to helping the displaced hobbits but also to replanting trees. The narrator points out that hobbits have been practicing for generations an indefinitely sustainable and healthy agriculture.

I could go on with examples for several pages discussing the hobbit approach to food, agriculture, and conservation—and indeed I have devoted a chapter of my book with Jonathan Evans, *Ents, Elves, and Eriador: The Environmental Vision of J. R. R. Tolkien* (University Press of Kentucky, 2006), to hobbit agrarianism. But maybe the best conclusion to all this is to cite the dying words of the dwarf-king Thorin—who because of his pride and lust for treasure had nearly caused a war between dwarves, elves, and men—spoken in repentance to Bilbo Baggins near the end of *The Hobbit*: "If more of us valued food and cheer and song above hoarded gold, it would be a merrier world" (ch. 18). Thorin, I think, was right; if we cared more about these things—about seed cakes and tea and fresh berries and cream, eaten in the company of friends—our world would not only be merrier; it would be a place of far less strife and one better taken care of. And that seems to be one of the central ideas in Tolkien's writing and one well worth considering, a vision of the good life that comes to readers like "bread, surpassing the savour of a fair white loaf to one who is starving": we need to care about what we eat and how we eat it, about how and where we grow it, and about the people with whom we eat it.

12 Hobbits, Heroes, and Football

by CHELLE STEARNS

EVERY SEPTEMBER BRINGS WITH it the anticipation of fall colors, new beginnings and, yes, the National Football League. A few years ago, I celebrated the start of the academic year by attending a Seahawks game here in Seattle. The day was gloriously warm and sunny, a prized commodity in the Northwest. It was the opening home game of the season, and there were lots of extra bells and whistles. There were fireworks and a flyover by two F-16 fighter jets. The Sea Gals (the Seahawks' cheer squad) were dancing, the music was blaring, and the crowd was yelling at the top of their lungs.[1] CenturyLink Field, the home of the Seahawks, has a reputation as one of the loudest stadiums in the NFL, so you can only imagine the wash of sound and excitement.

I was not there to watch the game. I am not really a football fan, and I can't remember the last time I watched an entire football game, live or on TV. I was there because my orchestra was playing in the halftime show, so we were there as guests. On that Sunday at the beginning of September, I felt like a stranger in a foreign land observing a strange ritual called "opening day festivities." It was as if I were experiencing American culture for the first time. What I saw was pure energy and emotion in the midst of competition, power, and sex. This was a raw American ritual. I was overwhelmed, and I began to wonder how Christianity could compete with this other Sunday rite. And since that sunny Sunday I have been asking myself an even more important question: what have Christians unwittingly imported into the church in the name of competing with such powerful cultural rituals?

---

1. As the Sea Gals ran onto the field and began dancing in their skimpy outfits, a friend of mine (who is the father of a young girl) leaned over to me and commented, "I wonder what their fathers think?"

Now, do not get me wrong. I think football is fine in and of itself. In fact, football was an important part of my family's holiday traditions—I can't remember a single childhood Thanksgiving or New Year's Day that didn't include watching long hours of football. Instead, what I'm working to understand is the ritual that surrounds the sport and how this ritual mirrors the evangelical Christian ritual.

The first similarity between Christian ritual and the ritual of professional football is that participants worship through the giving of some kind of monetary offering, whether it is in the form of buying tickets and team paraphernalia or through the charitable giving of tithes within the church. This type of financial sacrifice is required in order to be a full member and participant within the ritual. Of course, there are always people present that have not given money—such as my orchestra on that opening Sunday, who were guests of the Seahawks—but, in general, the offering of money is a sign of allegiance and loyalty, especially within a consumerist culture.

The second similarity follows from the first: we spend our money so that we can wear the group's required uniform. Every church has a kind of uniform, whether it is a suit and tie *or* shorts and a Christian T-shirt with flip-flops (the standard wear of the church I grew up in). Similarly, there is a consumerist identity for football fans. At the Seahawks game I attended there were many people wearing jerseys with their favorite player's name on the back. I, in contrast, wore a red shirt because I wanted to match my sandals (I'm such a girl.) This would have been just fine if the Seahawks (blue and silver) were not playing the San Francisco 49ers (red and gold—gulp!). As I walked around, I was confused by the glares that I received from many people. It wasn't until later that I realized my taboo; I was showing, through my lack of the ritual costume, that I was an outsider.

Third, ritual requires some voicing of praise. This kind of praise giving (cheering) looks very different in church than it does in a stadium, yet both require some kind of celebration or vocal acknowledgement that the team or God is worthy of our loyalty and sacrifice. Granted, church services are rarely as loud as a cheering crowd at CenturyLink Field, but I am merely suggesting similarities, not positing equivalent expressions of praise.

Fourth, both Christianity and professional football have a place for voicing complaint. There may be no official place within the performed ritual for lament and disagreement, but these reactions play vital roles in both football and the church. What would football be without a fan's dissatisfaction with a referee's call? And what would our relationship with God be like if we could not call out in our distress, "How long, oh Lord?" The freedom to complain demonstrates a certain amount of ownership or relationship. It signifies that the individual has praised and sacrificed and, as a consequence, expects something in return.

Finally, fans and congregations also identify leaders and heroes through whom they organize or perpetuate the ritual. Such heroes include the star quarterback, the burly linesman, the mascot, the pastor, the worship leader, and the missionary. They are the ones we hold up as our example and ideal. But if we are not careful, these persons become archetypes rather than people, celebrities rather than humble leaders. These are the people who miraculously live amazing lives or fall long and hard from their pedestals of veneration. And when this happens, they are banished from the ritual in disgrace.

It is this final category that I want to explore in more depth, because our heroes are crucial to how we tell the story of who we are, and I believe that a central aspect of any ritual is its defining narrative, that story of who we are and what we do. One of the fundamental characteristics that draws people to football is its epic story of the team. In many ways, football is the story of the heroes who have gone off to win glory on the field of battle. Commentators talk of players being "in the trenches" and play up the drama of competition as old rivals "go to war." As the fans watch and cheer, heroic feats are lauded and tragic injuries are mourned. In every game there is honor to be won and lost. And the heroes sometimes journey far from home only to return as the ultimate victors—Super Bowl champions! Hence, much of the ritual of football follows this narrative of the heroic team.

Likewise, in the evangelical tradition, the stories we tell tend to focus on a victorious Jesus who has conquered evil and forgiven our sins. In my childhood church, we often sang hymns such as "Victory in Jesus" or "I'm in the Lord's Army."[2] In youth group, we sang Keith Green's "Jesus Commands Us to Go" and Larry Norman's "I Wish We'd All Been Ready." The subtext was that we needed to be on the right side and be prepared to go and fight the good fight. In line with this, the heroes of the faith that were raised up by the leaders of my church were the missionaries who had traveled the farthest and into the most remote areas of the world in order to spread the gospel.[3] Following this example, the students who were thought to be the most mature in our youth group were the ones who sacrificed their summers to go on

2. I still remember marching around the pews in the sanctuary singing this song.

3. As a teenager, I was enamored by the story of Jim and Elisabeth Elliot, and by the way that Elisabeth had gone back to work with the tribe that had killed her husband and four other missionaries. I do not want to minimize the power of this story, but it is significant that Elisabeth soon came back to the states to raise her daughter. The majority of her life has consisted in teaching and writing, yet she is most widely known for being the widow of Jim Elliot.

mission trips to Africa or Papua New Guinea. Christian vocation was about spreading the good news; all other callings were secondary and secular.

It seemed in my youth that all teaching and discipleship was for the sake of sending out missionaries and telling the story to those who didn't know. I have heard a number of different pastors and youth leaders talk about life as a football game and church as the half-time break where we are rejuvenated and inspired to get back to the real action. What is strange is how this narrative diminishes the role and value of worship and the slow work of discipleship in the Christian life. Ecclesial life is thus reduced to a mere warm-up to the main events of evangelism and mission.

As we can see, how we tell the central story of the ritual influences how we live and what we value. Literary critic Northrop Frye argues that humanity tells two primary kinds of stories: (1) the story of the "warrior-hero" and (2) the story of the "homemaker," or what I call the "healer-hero."[4] The central narrative of the warrior-hero is one of exile—a time of earning glory *away* from home. There are noble journeys to embark upon and evil foes to vanquish. These tales elucidate the cunning and the skill of the warrior, the moments of glory and victory. Sometimes these are stories of ultimate sacrifice, where the hero dies but the battle is won. Other times, the warrior-hero wins the war and then weds the most beautiful woman as his reward. Thus, triumph ends in home and fertility, until the next adventure takes him away—action never takes place at home. However, it is the healer-hero who maintains the ordinary time of home life. These are the stories about where we live day to day. They focus on the slow growth of flowers, vegetables, and children. Time is slow and there is not a lot of action. All you have to do is think about your favorite chick flick to understand what I mean.

This dichotomy of the warrior-hero and the healer-hero is helpful for examining how we tell stories or act out such stories in our rituals. I contend that in our own stories, especially in the Christian story, the ideal is to find some kind of a middle way between these two kinds of heroes. Yet within evangelicalism, I see that an overemphasis on the victorious aspect of Jesus has led us to seek certain kinds of heroes over others. An exaggerated focus on Jesus as warrior, to the detriment of Jesus's other critical role of healer, has led us to raise up Christian heroes that, sadly, look far more like our sports heroes than the true hero of our faith. Another way of

4. See Northrop Frye's *Anatomy of Criticism: Four Essays* (Princeton, NJ: Princeton University Press, 1957); and *The Great Code: The Bible and Literature* (New York: Harcourt Brace Jovanovich, 1982). For an analysis of Northrop Frye's theory of the heroic story see Loren Wilkinson, "Tolkien and the Surrendering of Power," in *Tree of Tales: Tolkien, Literature, and Theology*, eds. Trevor Hart and Ivan Khovacs (Waco, TX: Baylor University Press, 2007) 73–74.

saying this is that we value the adventurous sacrifice of the extreme missionary over the little old lady who has faithfully served in the nursery for fifty years (or even the hardworking yet invisible organist).[5] Both examples are equally valuable, but not equally glamorous, and we would much rather be glamorous than faithful in a slow and steady manner. Only by holding together in tension the roles of warrior and healer can we discover the qualities that we should look for in our own heroes. Thus, I argue for a more humble sort of hero archetype: the gardener-hero.

THE STORIES WE TELL AND HOW WE PERCEIVE THE HERO

In self-consciously examining the way the Christian story is told, the goal should be to elucidate a fuller picture of Jesus, the central hero of the Christian story. Different traditions of the church have emphasized Jesus as either the warrior (i.e., the victorious conqueror over Satan, sin, and death) *or* the healer (e.g., what some critics have called the feminization of the church). But Jesus is both the warrior *and* the healer, and these two characteristics of the hero must be held in dialectical tension in order to understand who Jesus is as our hero. To that end, I propose the concept of the gardener as a means of exploring the paradox of the warrior/healer, and to aid my exploration I enlist the help of J. R. R. Tolkien's *Lord of the Rings* trilogy, a heroic tale highly influenced by Tolkien's own understanding of the Christian story.

The *Lord of the Rings* is one of the great epic tales of twentieth-century English literature, and since the movies came out a few years ago, it has found an important place within the popular imagination. It has everything one could want: complex characters, the struggle between good and evil, intrigue, mystery, danger, unexplored lands, romance, history, poetry, mythical swords, epic battles, magic rings, and, lest we forget, giant eagles (who always seem to save the day). Given this diversity of scope, it is no surprise that the idea of heroism is extremely complex within Tolkien's prose. In fact, the most obvious heroes, that is, the ones who acquire the greatest quantity of brave deeds and fame, are not ultimately the central heroes of the trilogy. As professor Loren Wilkinson argues,

> The real hero of the Tolkien story, as many have pointed out, is not Aragorn the king, or Gandalf the wizard, or any of the sword-bearing warriors. It is not even Frodo the Ring-bearer; it is rather Sam the gardener.[6]

5. Behind these examples are a few of the women who were important heroes from my youth.

6. Wilkinson, "Tolkien and the Surrendering of Power," 74. I owe much of my consideration of

Wilkinson points out that one of the vital characteristics of the *Lord of the Rings* is how it balances (or subverts) the story of the warrior with that of the gardener. Throughout the story, Sam the gardener maintains faith, hope, love, and courage because he remains true to the belief that he and Frodo will return home to the Shire; he realizes there is little glory in the heroic journey if there is no garden to return to and tend. One example of this is found in the film version of *The Return of the King* where, in the midst of Frodo and Sam's journey into the dark and barren lands of Mordor, Sam admits that his rationing of the elven way-bread is meant to sustain their journey to Mount Doom and then back home again.[7] Throughout the story, when Frodo has lost hope, Sam remains steadfast, even to the point of becoming a warrior in the necessary moments: Samwise Gamgee, slayer of the great Shelob and bearer of the light of Galadriel. Yet Sam's way is never guided by the narrative of one who seeks to find glory in battle. Instead, his defining narrative is that of the gardener who tends to daily needs of bread, water, and hope. And it is characteristic of Tolkien's overall vision of true heroism that the final words of the series come when Sam says, "I'm back."

Consider Galadriel's gifts to the members of the fellowship of the ring. The majority of the gifts given by Galadriel, the elf queen of the forest of Lothlórien, were for the purpose of surviving the journey that awaited the fellowship. However, Sam's gift is an exception. It is not for the journey but, instead, for the end—or we could say the beginning—of his story. She gifts Sam a small box containing the seed of a Mallorn tree and soil from the forest of Lothlórien.[8] Galadriel's gift enables Sam to heal the Shire after the ravages of war. Moreover, its purpose could only be revealed at his homecoming.

Sam is the true hero, even if he is not the most celebrated of the characters. He is the one who allows his love of Frodo and the Shire to guide him to the very end.[9] If we think back to Frye's categories of the warrior-hero and the healer-hero, then we

---

Tolkien's *Lord of the Rings* to insights drawn from Wilkinson's article.

7. In the books, Sam's longing for home is illustrated in subtle ways that are never as explicit as this scene in the movie.

8. In the books, it is very provocative that Sam never opens the box until he returns to the Shire. In the movie version, Galadriel instead gives Sam a rope. This is a significant though subtle departure from Tolkien's portrayal of Sam. In this move the movie undermines Sam's identity as the ultimate hero of the story, who is both warrior and healer. Similarly, the movies also miss the importance of Aragon's healing gifts, even though the books suggest that this is one of the signs that he is the true king of Gondor.

9. This motivation can be observed most poignantly when Sam refuses to use the ring to save Frodo from the orcs in the tower of Cirith Ungol:

can recognize that Tolkien's ultimate hero is both the reluctant warrior in exile *and* the healer who loves home—the one that can heal the wounds of war. Sam's story fits the typical warrior archetype in that he is triumphant away from home and then returns to marry his sweetheart, Rosie Cotton. But he also fulfills the healer archetype as he turns his heart and his action toward the slow growth of flowers, trees, and children. He is thus the gardener-hero because his story ends in domesticity and fertility, to the benefit of the entire Shire.

At the end of his exploration of Tolkien's gardener-hero, Wilkinson notes the similarities between Tolkien's story and the Christian story. He concludes that the balance between warrior and gardener within the Christian tradition is problematic and has often been misconstrued: we have overemphasized the warrior and forgotten the gardener in the story of salvation. In the process, we have overlooked the way that Jesus *surrenders* power in order to *win* the battle on the cross:

> For the Christian story too is about the centrality of surrendering power—indeed, about gardening. Not only does the story begin in a garden but at its climax, the hero returning from his underground journey is rightly mistaken . . . as a gardener. The unheroic gardener is the hero of Tolkien's story—and of the even greater Christian story that informs it.[10]

Hence, in the Christian story of salvation, Jesus's life also subverts the two dominant hero archetypes because he, like Sam, is both the warrior and the healer. However, he is able to be this kind of hero for us only through the surrendering of power.

WHAT KIND OF HERO IS JESUS?

The Christian story begins and ends in garden imagery. In the first garden story, we observe the origins of all of life as well as the sorrow of alienation from the Creator God. Thus, the first story tells of the fullness and potential of all life while at the same

---

He had only to put on the Ring and claim it for his own, and all this [Sam's version of power and glory] could be.

In that hour of trial it was the love of his master that helped most to hold him firm; but also deep down in him lived still unconquered his plain hobbit-sense: he knew in the core of his heart that he was not large enough to bear such a burden, even if such visions were not a mere cheat to betray him. The one small garden of a free gardener was all his need and due, not a garden swollen to a realm; his own hands to use, not the hands of others to command. (J. R. R. Tolkien, *The Two Towers* [London: HarperCollins, 1999] 206–7)

10. Wilkinson, "Tolkien and the Surrendering of Power," 83.

time explaining our poverty and need for redemption. The Christian story ends in a garden as well, or perhaps we should really say a garden city. Revelation 22 tells us of the healing power of the tree of life, and this is the consummation of God's redeeming work for all of creation.

Of course, in between these two garden accounts is the story of the incarnate Jesus, and it is in the person of Jesus that the final garden of healing is made possible. It is in his embodiment as both warrior and healer that he is able to bring about the redemption of all things. Thus, it is in understanding Jesus as gardener that we can begin to truly know what kind of hero Jesus is for us.

The Gospel of John recounts how the resurrected Jesus is mistaken as a gardener. When I think of John's version of the story, Rembrandt's rendition of the resurrection immediately comes to mind.[11] I love this painting. It captures something of the sorrow mingled with joy and surprise found in the resurrection story. No one really expected Jesus to come back to life, so how could they be prepared for such a wonderful shock?

In John's account, Mary Magdalene goes to the tomb only to find it empty. Upset and confused at her discovery, she then goes to tell the disciples what she has seen, and they all run back to the tomb. Then the disciples go home, but Mary stays, for she is bewildered and overcome with sorrow. No one seems to know what is going on. She remains weeping at the entrance to the tomb when two angels ask her why she is crying: "'They have taken my Lord away,' she said, 'and I don't know where they have put him'" (20:1–18).[12] It is at this point that a man approaches Mary, a man she believes is the gardener. This is the moment that Rembrandt captures in his painting. Jesus approaches her, with a broad hat and a gardening trowel in his hand. It seems that Rembrandt's Jesus is a bit playful as he acts the part of the gardener for Mary's sake. Jesus then reveals his true identity to Mary and she cries, "Rabboni!"

I believe that a significant characteristic of Jesus's personhood is revealed in this moment. Perhaps it is this idea that Rembrandt is playing with in this painting: that Jesus, the teacher, is also the gardener. However, he does not tend just a small plot of land but all of creation.

The vocation of gardening is multifaceted. Good gardeners know their plants and the soil of their garden. This intimacy allows them to tend and nourish the soil because plants cannot flourish in depleted ground. Part of this tending is discernment between what to plant and what to dig up. Every plant also grows in its own

11. View the painting at http://www.royalcollection.org.uk/eGallery/object.asp?object=404816.

12. All scripture is quoted from the NIV.

season, taking from the soil and giving back in its time. Good gardeners know the difference between what is thriving and dying or what is a weed and what is a plant in its proper place. This kind of tending requires daily diligence as well as a willingness to get one's hands in the dirt. To show Jesus with a gardener's hat with trowel in hand is a hopeful image for me. It shows that at the resurrection the work of redemption is near. A well-tended garden provides plenty of space for flowers, plants, and fruit to grow to fullness and maturity. And in this image, I see that redemption can take root and thrive.

The Son of Man is a biblical title that Jesus claims for himself that evokes the notion of being the gardener of all creation. The primary task of the Son of Man is to discern (or judge), to uproot, and to set things in order, much like a gardener must know his garden well enough so that he can discern the weeds from the other plants. One can argue that weeds are simply plants that are out of place, but in his parables, Jesus taught about the more detrimental characteristics of weeds. In his parable of the Sower, he warns that weeds will choke out the healthy plants, not allowing the soil to produce a good crop. Similarly, in the parable of the Wheat and the Tares, the weeds grow up among the crop of wheat (Matt 13:24–30). In this parable, the owner of the land is tempted to pull up the weeds immediately, but he fears the loss of his crop because the roots of the wheat and the weeds are intertwined. Thus, he waits until the time is ripe so that the wheat and the weeds can be separated properly without the destruction of the good crop. And in Matthew 15, Jesus rebukes the Pharisees for nullifying the word of God by preferring their traditions and laws to the commands of God. He warns them, "Every plant that my heavenly Father has not planted will be pulled up by the roots" (15:13).

It is clear from these passages that Jesus the gardener is given the task of separating the healthy plants from the detrimental influence of the weeds. Jesus is alluding to his role as the Son of Man, the one who will judge the whole created order on the day of judgment. It is often assumed that judgment is concerned primarily with condemnation, but many biblical accounts of judgment refer to it as discernment between the righteous and the unrighteous—such as the wheat and the chaff or the sheep and the goats. One will be preserved and the other will be—as stated in the parable of the Wheat and the Tares—tied up and burned (Matt 13:40–43). Thus, this is the eschatological role of discernment and setting right. Evil is not merely pruned back; it is entirely uprooted by the Son of Man on this day. As in Tolkien's tale, evil is undone.

From the image of Jesus as the one that uproots and conquers evil, we now turn to the image of Jesus as the one that provides healing and fecundity. This healing is only possible because evil has been uprooted; evil has no place or possibility in the garden at the end of things. In Revelation 22 we are given a vision of the river of the water of life that flows from the throne of God and the Lamb and runs down the middle of the New Jerusalem. On either side of this river is the tree of life, which is continuously fruitful and whose leaves are for the healing of the nations.

I can clearly imagine Jesus as the gardener of the New Jerusalem. The water of life flows from Jesus and sustains the tree of life. It is this tree that provides healing for the whole of the redeemed creation. Jesus is almost Bacchus-like—though he is filled with the water of life rather than wine—as he causes lush vegetation and fruitfulness to spring forth from everything that he touches.[13] Here and there he runs and leaps and in each place is fruit beyond imagination. Everything is healthy and his presence brings light and beauty to all things. Jesus the gardener spreads his glory wide and all people and every thing responds. This is the fulfillment of 2 Corinthians 3:18: "And we, who with unveiled faces all reflect the Lord's glory, are being transformed into his likeness with ever-increasing glory, which comes from the Lord, who is the Spirit."

Our transformation into the likeness of Jesus the Lord through the Spirit is the invitation given later in the chapter:

> The Spirit and the bride say, "Come!" And let him who hears say, "Come!" Whoever is thirsty, let him come; and whoever wishes, let him take the free gift of the water of life. (Rev 22:17; cf. Isa 55:1–2)

Lavish is the tending of this garden. The gardener has prepared an overabundance for those who dwell there, and never-ending is the water that nourishes and satisfies. Where there was once nothing, there is now life. Where there were weeds that destroyed and choked, there is now fecundity and freedom. The book of Isaiah is filled with imagery of streams in the desert that are turned into gardens as God proclaims,

> See, I am doing a new thing!
> Now it springs up; do you not perceive it?

13. I am thinking of a scene near the end of C. S. Lewis's *Prince Caspian* where Bacchus and his entourage frolic from place to place, setting ivy and other green things to grow in order to take down the bridge and then the buildings on the other side of the river. Everywhere they go in their merrymaking, new life springs; all is turned to green and all are healed. See Lewis, *Prince Caspian* (New York: Macmillan, 1951) 194.

> I am making a way in the desert
> and streams in the wasteland. (43:19)

Jesus makes a way for redemption for the sake of his glory and the glory of all people and things. And in the end, Jesus the gardener names all things good.

HOLDING TOGETHER THE UPROOTING AND HEALING ROLES OF JESUS THE GARDENER

In order to maintain a fuller understanding of Jesus, we need to hold together in a dialectical tension the concept of the victorious Christ, who is able to vanquish evil, with the concept of the healing Christ, who is able to make all things new. It is important to balance these two concepts because an overemphasis on one or the other leads to a misunderstanding of who Jesus is for us. On the one hand, an emphasis on the victorious Christ tends to lead our theology toward an overly triumphant and domineering God who has little space for our frailty and humanity. On the other hand, an emphasis on the healing Christ tends to lead us toward an assumption that love and healing is equivalent to blind acceptance and inclusion of all people, regardless of sin, or what one of my friends calls "holiness issues." Instead, we need a more robust middle way that combines the warrior and the healer in our understanding of the hero.

The concept of the gardener brings together these two ways of thinking about the work of Jesus for us. Somehow, thinking of Jesus as the gardener-hero leads us down the right path. Because that which has not been planted by the Father must be pulled up by the root (evil must be undone) in order for the healing waters to flow and for the leaves of the tree of life to go out to all the nations for healing. Jesus is both the warrior-hero and the healer-hero. His warrior role makes way for the possibility of healing, and healing fulfills the work of the warrior. These are mutually constitutive roles for Jesus. Jesus is the ultimate gardener-hero.

CONCLUSION

The way we tell the story is important because we are storytellers and story hearers. We are even story dwellers.

This reality is shown in how we dive into the ups and downs of our favorite teams. The narrative of victory and defeat pulls us along, and occasionally, when a great victory is won, entire cities full of strangers run out into the streets to hug one another and raise their voices in triumph. The story pulls them together in community.

This unifying power of narrative is what is most potent about football or any other team sport. It defines and it shapes entire communities. Loyalty is earned over time and jerseys are bought by fans because of the great accomplishments of the best players.

Although this is such a powerful force within our culture as storied people, we rarely stop to ask why and how we tell our stories. What we value shapes how the story is told. In football, what is most valued is the glory of winning, and Christianity often takes on this same narrative. The problem is that we belong to an upside-down kingdom; our values are different. Victory is not always about winning. Sometimes it is most profoundly about losing. Jesus surrenders his power, and it is in that reversal that redemption is made possible. The cross is a transforming subversion to the triumphant warrior story. And this transposed triumph leads to healing, which is the unraveling of evil—"Oh death, where is your sting?" The power that *defeated* Jesus on the cross is utterly incapacitated.

So in our telling of the Christian story and in how we form our communities through ritual, we must be aware of the fullness of the story of Jesus Christ who is the gardener-hero. We sometimes import things from our culture to help us tell the story, but as Tolkien has shown, the most obvious heroic traits are not always the most significant. We must continue to search out and express well the subtleties of the Christian story.

On a practical level, it is important to have a full picture of Jesus because, as the church, we are making disciples that are being conformed to the image of Christ. And if we are to be conformed to this image, we too must become gardeners. We fight for truth (a skill at which evangelicals excel), but we also must tend and bring health to all things around us. Our spiritual lives and communities must on some level reflect the gardener identity of Jesus. We must continuously strive to embody this story fully for the entire world to see.

And in the process, we may even watch a bit of football.

13 *The Tree of Life* and the Lamb of God

by PETER M. CANDLER JR.

IN ONE OF THE most astonishing passages in the book of Genesis, in the book's second creation narrative, the Lord God is depicted as a gardener, out for a leisurely evening stroll in the garden he has just made, clearly pleased with his creation. In fact, there is almost a sense in the text that God is so taken up by this delight that he appears to be distracted, lost in wonder for a moment. Between God's creation of Eve from Adam's side (2:23–25) and this scene (3:8ff), there is a pernicious and well-known interlude, upon which the rest of Scripture arguably depends. In this interlude, the crafty serpent famously introduces the first heresy: "you will be like God, knowing good and evil" (3:5). This subtly selective "truth" is the first instance of that perennial allure of the conspiracy theory. In effect, the serpent tells the man and the woman that God doesn't want them to know the "real" truth—in his selfish will-to-power Big Truth is really a Big Lie; he only wants to keep divinity to himself. Of course, as we all know, the first humans fall for it.[1]

It is surely meant to strike us that God, casually moseying through the garden, almost acts surprised when he sees the man and woman covered in leaves. What could possibly surprise God? "But the Lord God called to the man, and said to him, 'Where are you?' he said, 'I heard the sound of you in the garden, and I was afraid, because I was naked; and I hid myself.' He said, 'Who told you that you were naked?'" (3:9–11).

This scene is frequently described as the origin of an irreversible human tendency toward disobedience, as initiating a tragic chain of events that will eventuate in the sending of the Redeemer. According to this picture, God makes a beautiful world, and the first couple almost immediately screws it up. God then scrambles

---

1. Biblical citations are from the RSV except where otherwise indicated.

to come up with Plan B, which he brings to fruition by sending his Son to save his creation from our own inveterate capacity to make a complete, chaotic mess of it.

This is a caricature, it is true. But what makes this passage so challenging to much garden-variety theology of this sort is that it is not the good that surprises God but the sin. Sin emerges as the unaccounted-for thing, the unanticipated. The Lord God appears not to have foreseen that the vastness of his generosity would be refused or missed by his creation. It is the shame of sin, though, that in a way "surprises" God—encountering the fumbling attempt of Adam to explain himself and his new fig leaf number, God effectively responds, "You *what*?"

In this passage, sin is associated immediately with shame, with an incapacity to marvel at the gift of our innate dignity. Sin is like the loss of childlike wonder at the extravagance of God's gift, which is followed by an attempt to manage everything for ourselves. Surely, this luxurious expenditure of God—the gift of a share in his glory—is irresponsible, we think; better it were managed more maturely. In this sense, sin is *adult*, the prerogative of those who have "come of age" and now see the alleged truth behind the mask. But the first humans settle for an alleged truth that is altogether less radical than the truth of God's free gift in creation. As G. K. Chesterton puts it,

> Perhaps God is strong enough to exult in monotony. It is possible that God says every morning, "Do it again" to the sun; and every evening, "Do it again" to the moon. It may not be automatic necessity that makes all daisies alike; it may be that God makes every daisy separately, but he has never got tired of making them. It may be that He has the eternal appetite of infancy; for we have sinned and grown old, and our Father is younger than we.[2]

This is the irony of the term *original sin*: more often than not, our sin is profoundly, pathetically *un*original and derivative in the worst way.

We have "sinned and grown old," yet he who the Scriptures call the Ancient of Days is eternally young. And the youthful, divine capacity for delight and playfulness is at work in Genesis. After forming man from the dust of the ground, "the Lord God planted a garden in Eden, in the east; and there he put the man whom he had formed" (Gen 2:8). In fact, the word *Eden* means precisely this: *delight*. Bill Cosby once pointed out that God is content to call a universe of absolute originality and

---

2. G. K. Chesterton, *Orthodoxy*, in *The Collected Works of G. K. Chesterton* (San Francisco: Ignatius, 1986) vol. 1, 263–64.

beauty "good"; we aren't satisfied with anything less than "excellence." "Man invents; God creates," Cosby says, "Man invented an automobile, called it 'fantastic'; God did a tree, said it was 'good.'"[3]

This may seem a rather long way of getting around to Terrence Malick's recent film, *The Tree of Life*. But insofar as the film deals with the theme of the creation—especially as refracted through the book of Job—and insofar as its very title refers to Genesis, it seems to me that the film demands a particular way of reading, a kind of hermeneutic that would fit this highly enigmatic, personal, and singular film into some frame of reference. *The Tree of Life* sets the particular narrative of a family raising three boys in Waco, Texas, in the 1950s within a universal, cosmic narrative. The style is something like that of Augustine's *Confessions*, in which the bishop of Hippo retells the story of his life in the form of a prayer. When he has brought the chronology of his narrative up to the point of his conversion, Augustine—inexplicably to some readers—begins the story again at the beginning: Genesis. It is one of Augustine's several attempts to write a commentary on the first book of the Bible, none of which he ever completed. But this version is most telling for the way in which Augustine suggests that we only tell the truth about our own lives, our own stories, when we realize that they are already part of a cosmic story that begins with the completely unnecessary gift of creation from nothing. As with the *Confessions*, much of the script of *The Tree of Life* is in the form of prayer, making the film a kind of conversation between God and human beings.

The goodness (and, indeed, the playfulness) of creation, and sin as the refusal of a share in the divine glory—these, I think, are at least part of what this peculiar film is all about. The fact that the film might be impenetrable to many viewers is due partially to the unique cinematic signature of its author and partially to the fact that these themes are not as much a part of the imaginative landscape of our time as they are for the characters the film portrays. In this way, *The Tree of Life* opens up an aesthetic caesura between the universal goodness of creation and the particularity of human suffering: it discloses to us a vision of one family's life refracted through the story of the cosmos itself, which "declare the glory of God" (Ps 19:1 KJV). What transcends this caesura (incidentally, the film closes with a shot of a bridge, a figurative crossing of the caesura) is suggested by the title of the film itself and its central symbol.

3. Bill Cosby, "Genesis," *Those of You with or without Children, You'll Understand* (Geffen/Warner Bros., 1986). I regard this as one of the most profoundly insightful readings of Genesis 1–3, which uncommonly illuminates the humor inherent to the text.

That playfulness should be such an important theme in a film entitled *The Tree of Life* is no accident, given that the tree of life is an ancient symbol for Wisdom, who, personified in Proverbs, proclaims,

> The Lord created me at the beginning of his work, the first of his acts of old. Ages ago I was set up, at the first, before the beginning of the earth. When there were no depths I was brought forth, when there were no springs abounding with water. Before the mountains had been shaped, before the hills, I was brought forth; before he made the earth with its fields, or the first of the dust of the world. When he established the heavens, I was there, when he drew a circle on the face of the deep, when he made firm the skies above, when he established the fountains of the deeps, when he assigned to the sea its limit, so that the waters might not transgress his command, when he marked out the foundations of the earth, then I was beside him, like a master workman; and I was daily his delight, rejoicing before him always, rejoicing in his inhabited world and delighting in the sons of men. (Prov 8:22–31)

The tradition of Christian interpretation that grew up around this passage swiftly identified the person of Wisdom with Jesus Christ, as Augustine himself shows. The idea of wisdom—or better yet, the *person* of wisdom—in the Old Testament came to be understood as a kind of figure of Christ himself; the confession of Christ as the Wisdom of God appears already in Paul's First Letter to the Corinthians (1:24). And of course, the consequence of saying that Jesus Christ is the incarnate Son of God was that "by him were all things created, that are in heaven, and that are in earth, visible and invisible, whether they be thrones, or dominions, or principalities, or powers: all things were created by him, and for him: and he is before all things, and by him all things consist" (Col 1:16–17 KJV). In this confession, cited in the Epistle to the Colossians and probably going back (in some form) to the earliest disciples, echoes of the passage from Proverbs 8 are clearly evident.

Largely lost since the eclipse of patristic and medieval exegetical traditions, the sense of divine playfulness in the creation was not simply a fanciful or sentimental theological motif. On the contrary, the creation of the cosmos as a "pointless" act of divine Wisdom was for many interpreters of Scripture a peerless expression of the gratuity of divine art: that is, the *fact* of the universe itself is intelligible only as a gift of the God who is Love, who does not need his creation but who, as it were, desires it into being. And love, as Chesterton saw, is childlike in its capacity to exult in repetition, such that the goal of all creation could be understood as a kind of play. Indeed God, Proverbs suggests, is playfulness itself. The Jesuit theologian Hugo Rahner (brother of the decidedly more dour, "scholastic," and famous Karl) unfolded the theme of the *Deus ludens* ("God at play") with a remarkable clarity and simplicity. Problems of translation from Hebrew into Greek and Latin notwithstanding, he explained that the "mystical idea of the world Logos remained among the Greek Fathers of the Church,"[4] not least in Gregory of Nazianzus, who writes,

> For the Logos on high plays,
> Stirring the whole cosmos back and forth, as he wills,
> into shapes of every kind.[5]

For Augustine, the tree of life is a kind of sacrament, a sign that somehow makes present that which it signifies: "God did not want man to live in Paradise without the mysteries of spiritual things made present in material things. Man, then, had food in the other trees, but in the tree of life there was a sacrament." Augustine was witness to an already well-established tradition that identified the tree of life in Eden with Christ as the Wisdom of God: "Thus Wisdom, namely, Christ Himself, is the tree of life in the spiritual paradise to which He sent the thief from the cross."[6]

The Tree of Life opens with an epigram from the book of Job, God's familiar and somewhat salty response to Job and his friends: "Where were you when I laid the foundations of the earth?" This is an echo of God's question to Adam and Eve in the garden, "Where are you?" And this is a central theme of *The Tree of Life*: our inquisitions of God, however justified, are always posterior to God's prior interrogation of us. Augustine saw this in his *Confessions* when he realized that "I have become a question to myself."[7]

It is no accident, perhaps, that the central metaphors in both Augustine and Malick are trees and gardens: it is a pear tree that the young Augustine destroys with no good reason other than the love of destruction, an episode echoed in central character Jack O'Brien's smashing of a shed window, launching a toad into the

4. Hugo Rahner, *Man at Play*, trans. Brian Battershaw and Edward Quinn (New York: Herder, 1972) 23. See also the classic treatment by Johan Huizinga, *Homo Ludens: A Study of the Play-Element in Culture*, trans. R. F. C. Hull (New York: Routledge and K. Paul, 1949).

5. Gregory of Nazianzus, *Carmina* I.2.2, vv. 589–90, quoted in Rahner, *Man at Play*, 23.

6. Augustine, *The Literal Meaning of Genesis*, trans. John Hammond Taylor Ancient Christian Writers 42 (Mahwah, NJ: Paulist, 1982) vol. 2, 38 (8.4.8) and 39 (8.5.9).

7. Augustine, *Confessions*, trans. F. J. Sheed, 2nd ed. (Indianapolis: Hackett, 2006) 217 (10.33.50), echoing 4.4.9: *factus eram ipse mihi magna quaestio.*

stratosphere on a toy rocket, or, most tellingly, beating the trunk of a tree with a stick. It is in a garden that Augustine hears the voice of a small child telling him to "take and read,"[8] upon which he fatefully turns to the Epistle to the Romans. Gardening was also the answer given by Voltaire's Pangloss to the insoluble absurdity of human suffering and divine justice: "We must tend our garden." In a world bereft of divine glory, where self-interested and agonistic "nature" prevails, that is all we can do.[9]

But in *The Tree of Life* it is Mr. O'Brien's attitude to gardening that is most notable. Like many Texans, he is almost obsessively competitive about his lawn. We see him gardening in a small plot on his property, but more importantly, we see him instructing the young Jack (Hunter McCracken) in the laws of competitive gardening. In one difficult scene, he takes Jack through the yard, pointing out to him every weed he has failed to uproot, every bald patch where grass should be.

Like Job, O'Brien (Brad Pitt) is a righteous man, at least by conventional standards: "I never missed a day of work. I tithed every Sunday." But clearly this is not enough to secure O'Brien's, or Job's, life against the ravages of what appears to be divine indifference, or at least the human will to dominate, as when his ideas are stolen by a rival. When human "natures" come into conflict, someone loses. The book of Job calls into question the notion of the *lex talionis*, that interpretation of retributive justice summed up in the proverb, "an eye for an eye, a tooth for a tooth." Human righteousness does not, in Job or *The Tree of Life*, amount to a life free of suffering, nor is material prosperity a sign of divine favor.

But Mr. O'Brien is not all buttoned-down moral tidiness and tucked-in rectitude. He is possessed of an uncommon musical gift, an ability literally to *play* that, maybe unbeknownst to him, has the exemplary power to attract his eldest son Jack to do likewise. In one scene, while watching his father play Bach on the organ, young Jack gazes at his father with admiration and love far greater and freer than what the commands are able to compel. But perhaps because of Mr. O'Brien's failure to realize his own exacting standards of technical perfection in his own musical performance, he ultimately gives up, unlike his apparent hero, Arturo Toscanini, whom he praises to Jack for recording a performance sixty-five times before he was satisfied with it. Grace periodically interrupts the routine in the O'Brien household when the father jumps up from the dinner table to run to the turntable and air-conduct Brahms's

8. Ibid., 8.12.29.

9. Voltaire, *Candide, or, Optimism: A Fresh Translation, Backgrounds, Criticism*, trans. & ed. Robert M. Adams, 2nd ed. (New York: Norton, 1991) 75.

Fourth Symphony, recorded by Toscanini. His appeals to his children to hear are appeals he can only but occasionally heed in his own life, encumbered as he is by the invariable pressure to be "the big man." He appears to be driven by what the film ultimately shows to be a false ideal of "perfection," namely, a moral fastidiousness that occludes the all-pervasive gift of being. He has, as yet, no eyes with which to see this.

The way of O'Brien's wife is an alternative, one that effectively amounts to this: "You have heard that it was said, 'An eye for an eye and a tooth for a tooth.' But I say to you, do not resist an evildoer. If anyone strikes you on the right cheek, turn to him the other also" (Matt 5:38–39 NRSV). The entire film is set up by her monologue, which we hear as a voice-over to scenes from her early life, juxtaposed with flashes of the final vision of the film:

> There are two ways through life: the way of nature and the way of grace. You have to choose which one you'll follow. Grace doesn't try to please itself. Accepts being slighted, forgotten, disliked. Accepts insults and injuries. Nature only wants to please itself. Get others to please it too. Likes to lord it over them. To have its own way. It finds reasons to be unhappy when all the world is shining around it. And love is smiling through all things.

Wisdom delights—this could briefly sum up "the way of grace" in *The Tree of Life*. In a sequence near the beginning of the film, scenes of boys at play, running around the yard, playing hide-and-seek, tossing rocks, are accompanied by one of the most dramatic musical scores in the film, from the Czech composer Bedřich Smetana's *Má vlast* ("My Homeland"); the pastiche crescendos up to supper time, investing with an extraordinary *gravitas* the most mundane, and even useless, acts of human playfulness. The wisdom of children, as Chesterton pointed out, is their exultation in the pointless and the routine, and in this sense, childhood is a unique province of a particular kind of wisdom that is in a way more mature than the managerial wisdom of adulthood.

In *The Tree of Life*, each "way" corresponds more or less directly with each of the parents: nature to the father and grace to the mother. That this characterization fits with many people's experience, especially for those who came of age in the postwar years, is clear and obvious. But Malick also refuses to make each parent strictly correspond to these themes. Mr. O'Brien is not only a stern disciplinarian, but also an affectionate, even doting father. These two are not mutually exclusive, but ultimately Mr. O'Brien is incapable of the kind of intimacy that appears to be a special gift in his wife. For example, when Jack and his father reconcile, they see themselves almost fully reflected in each other; the elder O'Brien becomes vulnerable to his son in an unprecedented way. Then at an important moment in their exchange, he appears to want to say more. He pauses as if on the crest of a confession that will broker a true intimacy with his son, but he ultimately turns and slowly returns to the house.

O'Brien's great failing is not an inability to live up to the law but something of a different order. As he hauntingly confesses, "I wanted to be loved because I was great. The big man. Now I am nothing. I lived in shame. I dishonored it all and did not notice the glory. Foolish man." Sin—following the "way of nature"—is a refusal of the gift of glory. This is most profoundly captured in the figure of Mr. O'Brien, a gifted pianist and organist who forfeited his talent to become an oilman. He warns his son not to do likewise: "Don't do like I did. I dreamed of being a great musician. I got sidetracked."

This exhortation is immediately followed by a scene in church, during a sermon on Job, in which the preacher asks whether we are only willing to praise God when he shows us his face, not when he turns his back. The following shot is crucial. As the voice-over asks, "Is there nothing which is deathless? Is there nothing which does not pass away?" the camera turns to a stained glass window featuring the Christ of the *Ecce Homo*, bound in chains and staring out at the congregation. His inquiring gaze returns the question to us, but it also provides a kind of answer to the question, "Is there nothing which is deathless?" In effect, the answer is: behold the man. The bound and mocked Christ is the deathless logic of the universe. The only thing that does not pass away, this film seems to say, is represented in that window. All the rest withers and fades. The echoes of Paul's unfortunately all-too-familiar discourse on love in 1 Corinthians 13 is given a metaphysical dimension: withdrawing this conception of love from its oversentimentalization effected by thousands upon thousands of wedding rites, Malick restores it too to its proper place as the central act of a cosmic drama, a drama in which the Logos in whom all things are made is the same Christ who offers himself in superabundant love for the sake of the world.

∽

The scenes depicting the creation of the heavens and the earth are among the most arresting not only in this film but in any film in recent memory. One of these scenes early in the film is set to the "Lacrimosa," by Zbigniew Preisner, from the Polish composer's *Requiem for My Friend* (written for filmmaker Krzysztof Kieślowski). It is significant that Malick sets this text from the Requiem Mass alongside scenes of the creation. It is also a piece from a Requiem—this time that of Hector Berlioz—that closes the film, the "Agnus Dei." The entire narrative of the film is bracketed by these two pieces from the Latin liturgy for the dead. The "Lacrimosa" might seem an ill-fitting musical setting for the creation of the cosmos, but it also makes certain paradoxical sense, in that creation is ordered to eternal rest and perpetual light. And here in the "Lacrimosa," the theme of judgment is also paramount: it is in effect the musical counterpart to God's question to Job, which is the theological melody underlying the entire film. It also evokes a famous line from Virgil's *Aeneid*: *sunt lacrimae rerum et mentem mortalia tangent* ("the world is a world of tears and the burdens of mortality touch the heart").[10] The French painter Georges Rouault adapted these lines for a plate in his *Miserere*, a meditation on the Passion of Christ that reveals glory in and through the obedient love of Christ, even in suffering and death. "There are tears in the heart of things"—Rouault's affirmation of Virgil finds a place even in the Christian economy of salvation, insofar as the center of the Christian mythos is the paradox of divine glory radiating in the innocent suffering of a Jewish peasant. Accompanying the creation in Malick's film, the "Lacrimosa" echoes another Pauline theme, again from Romans: "the whole creation has been groaning in travail together until now" (Rom 8:22). Rouault echoes this theme in a specifically christological register in another plate from the *Miserere*, depicting Christ on the Cross and entitled, after Blaise Pascal, *Jésus sera en agonie jusqu'a la fin du monde* ("Jesus Will Be in Agony until the End of the World").[11]

Malick clearly wants to disabuse us of allegorical interpretations that would simply equate his characters and scenes with particular types or ideas—for all its christological resonances, the creation scenes have no one-for-one correlation with the incarnation. For her part, though, Mrs. O'Brien (Jessica Chastain) is clearly "full of grace." The Marian imagery, strongly present throughout, is especially poignant in the final lines of the film, where a wispy Mrs. O'Brien, flanked by two angelic figures, says, "I give him to you. I give you my son." This open transparency to the divine will is evocative of the Marian *fiat* that leads to our salvation: Mary's yes to God, her self-surrender to the absolute generosity of God. This is the precise opposite of "nature's" self-seeking. It is what the French call *disponibilité*, the formation of the soul to be so disposed to the divine will that it offers it its unhesitating consent.

10. Virgil, *Aeneid*, 486–87, translation from *Aeneid*, trans. Robert Fagles (New York: Viking, 2006) ll. 558–59, p. 63.

11. *Miserere*, plate 35, 1948. The quote from Pascal is from Fragments B of the *Pensées*, trans. A. J. Krailsheimer (New York: Penguin, 1966) no. 919, p. 313.

But this way of existence, this way of seeing, is hard-won for all the characters in *The Tree of Life*. Jack himself learns, only after injuring his brother in a foolish experiment with a BB gun, that grace is not earned but comes before even our own failures. Thus, he looks confusedly at his younger brother when, after his attempts to apologize to him, it is his brother's forgiving hand on his shoulder that communicates the undeserved grace that will heal Jack. He then repeats this gesture to others: to his younger brother (in an especially moving scene, during a move from their familiar home, when they touch hands through the window), to the neighbor burned in a tragic house fire, and finally, and most significantly, to his mother in the last scene. There are no reasons for these exchanges other than that they befit the order of creation as such—they are the only response we can offer for the nonnecessity of our own existence, for the claims of love that others make on us that we not only do not ask for but which literally bring us into being. Nonnecessity, then, names the order not just of grace but of nature itself: it is not simply that nature is violent and grace is peaceful; rather nature itself—understood here as all that is created—is the first gift of grace itself, and even the non-human order is prone to the unnecessary and unpredictable gestures of a primary, peaceable love.

It may be to disabuse us of at least one common understanding of nature that Malick depicts a scene in which an apparently injured dinosaur lies vulnerable in a riverbed. As a potential predator approaches, we fully expect that it will take advantage of this easy prey—after all, that's what so-called nature would be expected to do. But strangely and inexplicably, the would-be predator, after subduing his would-be victim, releases him, and goes on his way. This does not suggest that the order of necessity is overcome; dinosaurs will still hunt, kill, and eat each other. But it does show us that this film is thinking of what we commonly call *nature* in an unfamiliar way, as an arena of unexpected and unnecessary grace. That is, even the "natural world" is capable of expressions of mercy and the restraint of untrammeled self-preservation.

In the face of the death of her younger son, presumably R. L. (Laramie Eppler), Mrs. O'Brien is offered the comfort that "Life goes on. God gives and God takes away. That's the way he is." This bit of proverbial wisdom is accompanied by the familiar skyward shot through a tree, except this is the only time we see this shot through a tree that is bereft of leaves or fruit, implying the fruitlessness of this kind of wisdom in the face of death. At almost the same point in the film, the now-grown Jack, walking through the lobby of a Dallas office building, sees a small tree, supported by cables, growing in a concrete planter in the middle of an outdoor construction project. Even in the midst of this paved-over world, the cosmos's will to life remains irrepressible, vulnerable but not ultimately subject to mankind's regime of domination.

Clearly, the model of the nature-grace relation in *The Tree of Life* is not strictly identical to the formulation of this idea in the classical Thomistic tradition. Thomas Aquinas famously said that "grace does not destroy but perfects and elevates nature."[12] Malick pushes this idea further: not only does grace presuppose nature, but the reverse is also true—nature presupposes grace. There are some interpretations of Aquinas that suggest that grace is a kind of corrective to nature rather than its ontological completion, that grace crowns nature like a roof on a house. This interpretation of Aquinas is of course debated within academic theology, and in any event, Malick's posing of this relation suggests a different but not contradictory approach: that grace is prior to nature, that the creation of the cosmos is already an expression of divine generosity, one for which our proper response can only be a gratitude that is synonymous with obedience.

During the scene of the birth of the middle son, for example, there is a curious shot of a kind of underwater house from which a small boy escapes through an open door to the surface above. Here, biological birth is preceded by an image of baptism, the passage of life from a kind of watery grave into a more fully shared or participatory existence. Here, the dualism of matter/spirit is preemptively undermined: just as grace presupposes nature, baptism ontologically precedes biological birth, making grace in a way the metaphysical principle of the universe. Of course this does not necessarily suggest that baptism is reduced from a sacramental rite to a logical principle or that it is immanentized beyond sacramental recognition. Rather, it suggests that, for Malick, the conventional way of proposing the nature-grace relationship is backward. Grace always comes first; nature, second.

In this sense, nature is the surprise of God. But what Malick appears to mean by *nature* is not what we might think, namely, the whole realm of created reality that is not human, that domain of reality whose defense belongs to environmentalists and whose explanation to scientists. Rather in *The Tree of Life* nature is the will to self-love that characterizes every sinful human being. It is synonymous with "sin", and thus it is the really surprising thing for God, as this reading of Genesis suggests. Nature is precisely that for which Mr. O'Brien comes to realize he is culpable: "I dishonored it all. I forgot the glory." This is reinforced by the monologue of the young Jack as he wrestles with his Gollum-like duplicity. Citing Paul's Letter to the Romans,

12. *Summa Theologiae*, Ia.1.8 *ad* 2.

Jack says, "I do not do what I want, but I do the very thing I hate" (Rom 7:15). He goes on: "Father, Mother: always you wrestle inside me. Always you will."

On the other hand, to the degree that Malick shows nature as the domain of human violence and unfreedom, his vision of grace gives back to nature a capacity to disclose the divine radiance. So Mr. O'Brien follows the way of nature as represented by his interpretation of the idea that "you can't be too good in this world." Read in this way, you can never be too good, because "The world lives by trickery." That is to say, if you want to get anywhere in this world you have to follow its rules. You can't be too proud to indulge in a little trickery yourself; the good people are not the successful ones. But read a different way, you can never be too good, because the good is infinite and inexhaustible, and you can never respond adequately to the miracle of its self-donation. The way of nature and the way of grace might, therefore, be two ways of understanding the idea that you can't be too good in this world.

This evokes an ancient question, dramatized in the myth of the Ring of Gyges in Plato's *Republic*, where Socrates asks, "Why be just?"[13] For Malick it appears that the only way to pose and respond to that question is by asking that most fundamental of metaphysical questions, "Why is there something rather than nothing?" The moral question is intelligible only within a much larger story, a "story before we can remember"; therefore being good is not a matter of accounting your moral debts and credits in calculus but primarily a response to the utter gratuity of the universe itself, to God's extravagant gift of life to which all being save mankind naturally proclaims. You can never be too good, because the good is infinite.

ᕤ

I suspect many readers of this film will take the first verse of the epigram from Job as the hermeneutical key to understanding the film. But Malick's decision to extend the epigraph beyond that verse seems instructive: after citing the familiar rebuttal of God in Job 38:4, he jumps to verse 7, which is lesser known. The whole epigram thus reads:

> Where were you when I laid the earth's foundation? While the morn-
> ing stars sang together and all the sons of God shouted for joy?

This vision of an original harmony to the creation is a common theme in the Wisdom-inflected tradition of christological reflection: the cosmos is the expression of a divine and eternal Trinitarian harmony called "Wisdom," and as such, all nature

13. See Plato's *Republic*, esp. book 2.

rejoices in it. This is not to deny the inescapable drought occasioned by human sin but to understand sin as a refusal of the share in God's own glory offered by God in creation: in effect, Adam exchanged the glory he was freely given for self-imposed bondage that masqueraded as liberation. In so doing, we chose the tree of knowledge over the tree of wisdom and life, technical mastery over obedient gratitude. And even the mists are wiser than we. God's question to Job remains: "Who has put wisdom in the clouds, or given understanding to the mists? Who can number the clouds by wisdom?" (Job 38:36–37).

The sum of Malick's vision has a deep affinity with that of Gerard Manley Hopkins:

> The world is charged with the grandeur of God.
> It will flame out, like shining from shook foil;
> It gathers to a greatness, like the ooze of oil
> Crushed. Why do men then now not reck his rod?
> Generations have trod, have trod, have trod;
> And all is seared with trade; bleared, smeared with toil;
> And wears man's smudge and shares man's smell: the soil
> Is bare now, nor can foot feel, being shod.
>
> And for all this, nature is never spent;
> There lives the dearest freshness deep down things;
> And though the last lights off the black West went
> Oh, morning, at the brown brink eastward, springs—
> Because the Holy Ghost over the bent
> World broods with warm breast and with ah! bright wings.[14]

Malick's film is a work of *mythopoesis*, a work that reinscribes all particular stories within a single story of the created cosmos at whose center is the self-offering of the Lamb of God. This is powerfully illustrated in the final, enigmatic scene. In what is evidently some kind of heavenly dream vision (but not, it seems, a vision *of* heaven) for the elder Jack, he approaches a doorway with his mother, through which together they send the younger brother. Placing his hand on his mother's shoulder, Jack repeats the gesture he learned from his brother, thus fulfilling the latter's call to him at the beginning of this vision—"Follow me"—and completing the circle of reconciliation. This door image recurs a number of times, evoking John's gospel, which

14. Gerard Manley Hopkins, "God's Grandeur," in *The Poems of Gerard Manley Hopkins*, ed. Robert Bridges and W. H. Gardner, 3rd ed. (Oxford: Oxford University Press, 1948) 70.

returns to the pastoral theme that "I am the door: by me if any man enter in, he shall be saved, and shall go in and out, and find pasture." (John 10:9 KJV). Only after Jack's own passage through the doorframe into the desert before him does the arid and desperate salt waste become awash and fertile again, the site of reconciliation. At this point, Mrs. O'Brien, surrounded by two angelic figures, raises her hands to the sky, saying, "I give him to you. I give you my son." Spreading her hands apart, the blinding sun washes out the screen. The camera then descends to a shot of a field of sunflowers in which the image of the sun is, as it were, repeated infinitely in organic life. Put another way, the eternal Son is repeated infinitely in his creation, as a type and figure of the reconciliation of heaven and earth already effected in the self-gift of the Son. As Saint Paul writes to the Colossians, "It was the Father's good pleasure for all the fullness to dwell in him, through him to reconcile all things to himself, having made peace through the blood of his cross; through him, I say, whether things on earth or things in heaven" (Col 1:19–20).

The final sequence of *The Tree of Life* is set to the splendid final movement of Berlioz's Requiem (*Grande Messe des Morts*), the *Agnus Dei*. "The Lamb of God" theme brings us back to the *Ecce Homo*. In John's gospel it is Pilate who, presenting Christ bound to his accusers, says, "Behold the Man," as a kind of unwitting response to the words of John the Baptist at the beginning of John, "Behold the Lamb of God, who takes away the sin of the world" (John 1:29). In the Christian tradition, this Lamb of God is the reality of the figure of the tree of life planted at the center of the garden, with the signs of whose eternal grace "the world is charged" and which, imaged by the sun in Malick's film, "flame[s] out, like shining from shook foil," through the branches of the tree of life. And Berlioz's repetition of the phrase *et lux* ("and light") reinforces the ineradicability of light perpetual, even in this dark world, where "the darkness has not overcome it" (John 1:5). The image of the Lamb of God, the Light of the World, is the image of the way of grace itself, on whom "Generations have trod, have trod, have trod," have "seared with trade; bleared, smeared with toil." And yet: "for all this, nature is not spent."

∽

The fact that *The Tree of Life* is set in Waco, Texas, is significant not only because it is Malick's hometown but also because it has for some years now been something like the butt of a national joke. Widely assumed to be a breeding ground for freakish cult leaders and Bible-thumping preachers, its national and international reputation is not entirely undeserved. Yet we—especially those of us who live in Waco—have reason to be grateful to Malick for making his birthplace appear something different than the received image. He manages to disclose the beauty of the place by constant reference to its two most abiding features: the live oak and the sun. The former is the great glory of the southern United States and the most beautiful, hardy, and long-suffering of trees. The latter is searing and inescapable. Both are ubiquitous, and the union of them in the familiar shot of the gnarled and knotty limbs of live oaks irradiated by the sun is a kind of figure for the splendor of the divine light of grace that perfects and completes nature.

After seeing *The Tree of Life* for the second time, in Waco, my wife and I returned to the bright world from the theater at just the time when many of the shots in the film were made—the long twilight before sunset, when the sun is low and hot in the sky. As we walked through the parking lot, a shot right out of *The Tree of Life* opened before us: the low, diffuse sun flecked through a row of crape myrtles. This kind of image, usually shot from the ground to the sky, through a live oak, is one of the most prominent in the film, and seeing it this time was like seeing it through Malick's own vision, as a kind of sacramental sign of the glory of God shot through the tree of life.

To effect such a transformation of vision is arguably the goal of all true art, and this is the deeper reason why the choice of Waco is no accident. It takes vision to see this widely perceived cultural backwater as a locus of divine glory, and one cannot simply will oneself to see in this way. This is perhaps why the "eyes of faith" are "infused," as it were, as a genuine gift of God, an act of undeserved grace that makes one capable of seeing the world as "charged with the grandeur of God." Even Job has to learn how to see this way. That grandeur is, in Malick's film, made visible for its own sake through this bright and broken world's creation in and through the Son, repeated infinitely in every thing God deigned to call "good." To see with the eyes of faith, then, is to see that "love is smiling through all things." This brings Malick's vision very close to that shared by Saint Augustine, Maximus the Confessor, Hopkins, Dostoevsky ("beauty will save the world"), Sergius Bulgakov, and Dante ("the love that moves the sun and the other stars"),[15] a vision that is perhaps most eloquently articulated by the fourth-century saint, Ephrem the Syrian:

15. See Maximus the Confessor, *Maximus Confessor: Selected Writings*, trans. George C. Berthold (Mahwah, NJ: Paulist, 1985); Maximus the Confessor, *On the Cosmic Mystery of Jesus Christ: Selected Writings from St. Maximus the Confessor*, trans. Paul M. Blowers and Robert Louis Wilken (Crestwood, NY: St. Vladimir's Seminary Press, 2003); Fyodor Dostoevsky, *The Idiot*, trans. Richard Pevear and Larissa Volokhonsky (New York: Vintage, 2003); Sergius Bulgakov, *The Comforter*, trans. Boris Jakim (Grand Rapids: Eerdmans, 2004) 279f; Dante, *Paradiso*, 33.145.

Perhaps that blessed tree,
The Tree of Life,
Is, by its rays, the sun of Paradise;
Its leaves glisten,
And on them are impressed
The spiritual graces of that Garden.
In the breezes the other trees
Bow down as if in worship
Before that sovereign
And leader of the trees.[16]

16. Ephrem the Syrian, *Hymns on Paradise*, trans. Sebastian Brock (Crestwood, NY: St. Vladimir's Seminary Press, 1990) 90 (2.2).

14 Above Them All a Cherry Tree

by CHRIS ANDERSON

Behind the Monastery of St. Gertrude's
the Stations of the Cross climb a forested hill,
fourteen of them, plaster scenes
with wooden frames and shingled roofs
like small, flat houses
spread out along a path all the way to the top.
But they begin in an orchard, a cherry orchard,
and when I was there it was harvest time.
Jesus Condemned for Us,
the first scene read, in Gothic,
the Lord before Pilate, white as frosting,
the crowd on either side, standing in rows.
Above them all a cherry tree,
the hanging branches thick with fruit.
Bright red fistfuls of Bings.

15 Brunch and Foolishness

by A L I S S A   W I L K I N S O N

T HE WORD *BRUNCH* IS utterly stupid, and New Yorkers self-consciously es-
chew stupid things, as if it's their contribution to civilization. But if you ever
move to New York, you'll be standing at a party and a slightly tipsy someone will forcefully declare to you, bright-eyed, waving a rum and Coke, that
"New Yorkers love brunch."

You'll think about how pretentious that statement is, and then you'll start to notice that pretty much every restaurant in Manhattan and Brooklyn serves the same
menu from ten o'clock to two o'clock, sometimes until four, on weekends. The magi-
cal brunching hour.

And soon you too will become a New Yorker, and you too will love brunch,
with its unembarrassed menus of upscale hangover cures (ever-more-inventive up-
grades on the spicy Bloody Mary, fluffy feta-stuffed omelets, french toast stuffed
with mascarpone, big grilled cheese sandwiches with Parma ham) and its air of relaxation. For what could be more indulgent, more civilized, more lap-of-luxury than
lazing at a sidewalk table with your sunglasses and your comfortably chic sweater
dress and four friends laughing nearby, or your husband and a book and a bottomless cup of passably good coffee?

Of course I knew the word *brunch* before I moved into Greenwich Village, the
languid seat of haute civilization, but I grew up in the suburbs and then on a plot
of land out in the country, daughter of the working class, and we didn't do brunch,
except maybe on Christmas Day. We did breakfast (eggs and toast) and lunch (soup
and grilled cheese) and dinner (chicken and potatoes), and sometimes a bedtime
snack (popcorn). *Brunch* was just a funny word for breakfast when you slept in really

late. Or something at Grandma's, in pajamas, after sleeping over with cousins: chocolate chip pancakes, sausages, hot chocolate.

I can't remember my first brunch that first summer in New York, but by early fall I'd fallen in with a rotating group of acquaintances and a core cast of friends: one with a gorgeous apartment and the rare, coveted commodity of a table to eat at, one who worked in commercial realty and had inexplicably been to cooking school, a student at a design school nearby, a filmmaker, and, somehow, me.

The glorious lazy times we spent around that table, midday, with pear tarts, and roasted chickens and whole fishes, and buckwheat pancakes, and bottles of wine and good bread. We were grown-ups, all on equal footing despite the spread of age and education and experience between us. We could leave the scraps on the table and go down the street to Film Forum for a matinee. We could boldly start our meal with fresh orange-scented chocolate chip cookies, or watch through the north-facing wall of windows as the sun crossed from east to west, past the Chrysler Tower, behind the Empire State Building, and through the West Side's trees. We let the day fade away, together, in glorious companionship, confident nothing could change our world.

Ridiculous, really: a year later we'd all be headed in separate directions, one to Seattle to marry and settle down, one to DC to save other corners of the world, one home for the summer once classes ended, and then two of us, just the filmmaker and me, moving from Manhattan to Brooklyn to make a life for ourselves together.

⌐

Planning our wedding reception, we chose brunch, with french toast and scrambled eggs and biscuits and gravy (a nod to my in-laws' roots in backwoods Virginia) and apple crisp (a nod to my roots in Yankee country) and good coffee. "Everyone loves brunch," we said by way of explanation.

Then Dad died, very suddenly, too soon, and we canceled the brunch. Sometimes I still think about all those eggs and the bread and the gallons of syrup, and I imagine that brunch and what it would have been like. If it would have been any good. If I, too clumsy to wear white, would have dripped syrup on my dress. If we had invited someone who was gluten intolerant and forgotten to put something wheat-free on the menu. If people would have gone away pleased.

What we did, in the end, was transform the sandwich platters my in-laws had ordered for our rehearsal dinner into our wedding meal, laid out under a tent in the backyard where we married a couple days after we'd planned, and concluded it with cheesecakes. An awkward meal to celebrate the beginning of a marriage, which is, in turn, always a foolish proposition, no matter how you look at it. Check any New York restaurant's weekend menu: lunch food is brunch too.

⤳

Nobody seems to know where the foolish word came from—a portmanteau of breakfast and lunch, obviously, but we don't say *lupper* or *dunch*. Someone claims a reporter for the *New York Morning Sun* coined it in the early twentieth century as a way to describe the way a morning newspaperman ate: frenzied, I suppose, too busy to eat breakfast.

I gave up breakfast a long time ago, when I realized it just makes me hungry for lunch hours too early, but I think that portmanteau-inventing reporter and I, teaching college freshmen to wrangle words in the early mornings, are kindred souls. My students note on evaluations that I become more animated by the bottom of my coffee cup, and my midday classes pepper their evaluations with comments about my snacking choices. I gather their comments at the end of the semester and spend a happy hour laughing my way through them, seeing the shape of my semester through their eyes.

This job of mine is a silly undertaking. It pays very little and requires too much work and more than a bit of hand-wringing, and it asks me to invest into kids who will sometimes break my heart and sometimes make me love them, but while they think college goes on forever, I know they'll be gone in a few years anyhow. Like the newspaperman, I only eat brunch anymore, and sometimes linner, or maybe just a late-night snack.

⤳

Wall Street melted down while I stood in a pizza joint late one night on the Upper East Side with my husband, eating a slice and listening to the radio. We'd been at the Ninety-Second Street Y for a celebration of Maurice Sendak's eightieth birthday, the sort of star-studded affair you start to take for granted here, and when we stopped to eat, we realized that Lehman Brothers had basically disappeared while we were inside.

My husband was working in film and I had just quit my full-time job to work for two nonprofits, and I was suddenly terrified that I'd be laid off and we'd be destitute, and as I choked my way through the rest of the pizza and then into the next two months, I worried endlessly. I had done a very silly thing—quitting a good job that paid my graduate school tuition to chase a dream. I was choosing to play with ideas and artists over the steady work I was trained to do.

But for now, we had an income. Our friends: not so lucky. Each week, more became unemployed or underemployed.

Sitting one day in church, praying to know how to help, I realized that there was at least one thing I could do: I could make a meal and invite everyone we knew. At least they'd get a square meal. The first month, a dozen people showed up. The next month, fifteen. A year later, the group had grown so large we could hardly cram everyone into our five hundred square feet of studio apartment; friends sat on the chairs and the edge of the bed and spilled onto the floors and into the hallway.

Sheer idiocy, when you think about it. Figuring out how to feed a group of an unpredictable size requires time I don't have, skills I never acquired, and a couple of extra pots and burners.

⌒

Our church meets at eleven in the morning, and our liturgy positions the Eucharist near the end, so each week we serve the bread and wine around twelve fifteen. I rarely eat before the service, and I am hungry by then, and I frequently remember Paul's admonition to the Corinthians that folks ought not to partake in the most sacred of tables seeking to fill their stomachs. But the bite of pita bread and gulp of wine isn't stomach filling. And it leaves me thinking—always, and often so soon it reminds me of my mortality—of brunch: both what we'll have when the service concludes, and that this thing I do, this sacred meal in which I partake each week, like brunch, looks profoundly foolish from two paces away.

I watch as people line up to partake, and I know I have little in common with these people, and they have little in common with me. We'd never meet if we never came within these walls. The meal we're about to share is not good: inexpensive wine and semi-stale pita from the corner grocery. And yet we return to it every week, in the middle of the day, on a Sunday, when the rest of the city sits at sidewalk cafes. We line up in celebration and solemnity and tell each other that *this is Christ's body, broken for you; this is Christ's blood, shed for you,* and we know we're a bit mad.

But two paces in, standing to receive this unlikely meal with this unlikely family, the foolishness is sweeter than whatever meatball sliders or panini or flapjacks await me, sweeter than the coffee I need, sweet enough to keep me from pushing away what looks foolish to the wondering world.

16 Food as *Physis*: Homer and the Elements of Christianity

by DAVID WILLIAMS

FOOD AS *PHYSIS*

FOOD IS PRIMAL, AND the way in which we see the literal taking in of the inanimate, the recently animate, and the sort-of-animate says a great deal about how we see the world and our place in it. Christians are foodies by necessity. We worship a God who offers himself as food (the Bread of Life) and the ritual that sits at the center of our faith involves us eating that God whose body was broken for us.

I was first struck by the elemental and primal nature of this practice when my three boys were quite small. The congregation was being prepared to receive Communion, and to keep their wriggling to a minimum, I had all three seated on my lap. As the requisite Scripture was read, words like *flesh* and *blood* and *bone* took on new meaning as tiny and delicate rib cages pressed against my arm and hearts beat in the flesh of my own flesh. What father could not think anew of sacrifice and of Christ's body broken? The elemental and primal nature of this rite that I so often take for granted is an articulation of what is most basic about the world.

What I mean by "most basic" is what Thales (the first scientist in Western history) meant when he declared that everything is water. He did not mean, of course, that our impressions of the world are completely wrong, that there are no dry things, for example. What he meant was that if there were a single principle that could unify metaphysically and explanatorily the nature (*physis*) of the cosmos, then that one principle would be water: what living thing does not require water? What comes to be without water? In declaring the cosmos to be water, he was declaring that it possessed a fundamental *physis* (the Greek word that we translate "nature") that provided the interconnected key to all things. The ancient Greek scientists worked out their physics/physis in terms of the basic elements of earth, air, fire, and water. We followers of Christ have blood and bone, but rather than theorizing about the basic constituents of the universe, we eat them. The problem is that we don't always agree on exactly what we are eating, and therein lies the rub.

The food of the Communion table denotes a kind of physis because it indicates how we view the fundamental elements of the world: food as physis. While all Christians would agree to the centrality of this meal and that it sits at the heart of our faith practice as Christians, we are in serious disagreement over the ontological status of the bread and the cup. We disagree about the physis that is revealed by the Communion table. If I were a Catholic believer taking the Eucharist, I would see the real presence of the blood and body of Christ as literally "in" the elements of the table (this view is called "transubstantiation"). While there are more Protestant views on the sacraments than one can shake a stick at, chances are that the average Protestant does not see the Welch's grape juice in a plastic shot glass and its accompanying cracker as containing the real presence of the blood and body of Christ. Rather, the elements of the table are seen as symbolically pointing to the higher realities, but not containing them. The question I would like to ask concerns why we have these different stories. Why does roughly one half of Western Christianity take the physis of the elements of the table to be one thing, while the other half takes it to be another?

Answering these questions definitively is beyond the scope of what can be accomplished here, but I would like to highlight two disputes that figure into the story of Western Christianity. The first dispute is well known, the latter less so. I hope that by articulating these disputes we can as Christians frame our own dispute more clearly, with greater humility, and with an eye to how our cherished religious traditions interact with the cultural traditions from which they originate.

DISPUTE 1: PLATO AND ARISTOTLE

How did Western Christians come to see the elements of the table differently? Why do some think that the physis of the bread and cup consists of the actual blood and body of Christ, whereas others think that the elements of the table only symbolize (i.e., do not embody or contain) the actual blood and body of Christ?

If one has ever taken a philosophy course or perused the philosophy section at a large chain bookstore, it is very likely that one has been exposed to the Renaissance painter Raphael's masterpiece, *The School of Athens*. Countless publishers choose this image for the covers of their introductory anthologies, and it is ubiquitous on philosophy department websites and departmental propaganda (this author feels compelled to admit that he has overused it in nearly every applicable context). *The School of Athens* was completed between 1510 and 1511 as a part of Raphael's commission to decorate the rooms in the Vatican's Apostolic Palace with frescoes. The reason this image is so beloved by philosophy professors and introductory textbook editors is clear: it portrays one of the most important philosophical disputes in the history of Western thought with the kind of colorful imagery that philosophers can only dream about with their locutions. In the painting, all the great luminaries of classical Greek thought are present, but at the focal point of the painting one finds the two giants of Western philosophy, Plato and Aristotle, engaged in a debate. We find Plato cradling his work *Timeaus* in his left hand while gesturing heavenward, index finger extended, with his right. Meeting Plato's gaze, Aristotle holds his *Nicomachean Ethics* in his left hand while countering Plato's heavenward gesture with his right arm outstretched and palm downward as if to say, "But what about right here?"

Plato and Aristotle's dispute is quite complicated but it boils down to this: where does one find the good stuff? Are the formal and explanatorily relevant properties of the cosmos apprehended by transcending the sensory world (as shown by Plato's vertical gesture toward the world of Forms that exists beyond the sensory world)? Or is the metaphysical address of those formal properties found within the sensible world itself (as shown by Aristotle's horizontal gesture toward the phenomena of intelligible principles to be found through empirical investigation)? What both student and teacher agree upon is that the world is, in fact, intelligible. In other words, that intelligible principles exist which allow us to explain the world is not under dispute; Plato and Aristotle merely disagree about the location of formal intelligibility and the method one should use to apprehend it. For Plato, one needs to move beyond the senses to the Forms, whereas for Aristotle, all knowledge begins with the senses.

What the introductory philosophy textbooks and departmental advertising seem to leave out, however, is that *The School of Athens* is intended to elucidate a theological difficulty particular to the Christian faith. *The School of Athens* fresco was painted on a wall in the *Stanza della segnatura* ("Room of the Signature"). On the opposing wall of this room, where the Pope signed important documents, was the *Disputa*, which depicts a debate over the nature of the Christian sacraments. The two paintings were meant to be viewed together: one could stand in the room and see on one wall the dispute between Plato and Aristotle and on the opposite wall the dispute over the sacraments.

In the *Disputa*, we have a crowd of theological luminaries, but at the focal point we find the mirror image of the gestures employed by Plato and Aristotle. In this painting, however, the dispute is over the nature of the sacraments and their metaphysical status. On the one hand we have a figure employing the gesture used by Plato to indicate that cup and bread of the table are merely symbolic; their true reality lies elsewhere. According to this view, the bread and wine point to, or symbolically represent, the blood and body of Christ. On the opposite side of the table we find a figure making the horizontal gesture of Aristotle to indicate what will become the orthodox Catholic position of transubstantiation: that the true realities of the body and the blood are found *within* the mundane composites of bread and wine. According to this view, when the elements of the table are consecrated, they may maintain their appearance as bread and wine, but their true reality or substance is altered, actually becoming the body and blood of Christ.

Raphael's paintings, completed before the Reformation hit its full stride, prefigure the basic metaphysical positions between each respective side: the Catholic position will come to accept that the sensible properties of this world can actually bear the divine presence, whereas the Protestants will eventually agree to the basic idea that the elements of the table point to but do not contain the metaphysical robustness of the actual blood and body of Christ.[1] This dispute has implications far beyond the nature of the sacraments and affects everything from differing perspectives on the role of art in worship (compare virtually any Catholic church to your average Protestant church in terms of how they are outfitted to incorporate visual art into the worship experience) to reproductive ethics (compare the Catholic concern regarding birth control to the Protestant lack of concern regarding birth control). This debate is crucial because it is essentially a dispute about the human being's relationship to the sensory world: Can the sensory world deliver the goods or not? Are we people of Aquinas's notion of natural or general revelation? Or are we a people of Luther's *sola scriptura*?

1. Detailing each Protestant position, from Luther's less than straightforward assertion that the real presence of the body was "behind" the elements rather than "in" the elements as the Scholastics had held, to the Anabaptists' straight-up symbolism, is beyond the scope of this essay. For the sake of simplicity, I here assume that Protestants take the Platonic side of Raphael's visual representation, whereas Catholics take the Aristotelian side.

Arguably the most fundamental relationship that we have to the world of the senses revolves around food. It is literally an ingesting of *nature* three (or more) times a day. What one thinks about food follows from one's metaphysics. Raphael got it right: Plato and Aristotle set out the metaphysical positions that would be ultimately adopted by Christian theologians—Catholics rely more heavily on the Aristotelianism found in Aquinas, with Protestants finding the Platonism transmitted through Augustine (as read by Luther and Calvin) more useful. However, Raphael should have added a third painting, one that would help shape why Plato and Aristotle disagreed. And this third painting would get us even closer to the notion of food as physis. This third painting should have been of Odysseus and Achilles arguing over when to have lunch.

DISPUTE 2: ACHILLES AND ODYSSEUS

What do Achilles and Odysseus have to do with the sacraments? Raphael's visual argument is that debates in Christianity are often influenced by views and positions outside of Christianity itself. But what of Plato's and Aristotle's views? What prefigures their metaphysical positions? Here is the claim that I wish to make: the positions of Plato and Aristotle are prefigured in Homer, and the metaphysical options that they stake out are actually embedded in the debate between Achilles and Odysseus in Homeric epic. If I am right, then our debate as Christians over the sacraments is influenced not only by Greek philosophy, but also by the first and most important works of Western literature. I am not claiming that Plato and Aristotle consciously read Homer and formulated their metaphysical positions accordingly. Plato and Aristotle (as well as the Gospel writers writing in Greek) imbibed Homer as they would mother's milk. The Homeric view of the world was so deeply embedded in antiquity that it constitutes the backdrop against which conceptual developments in philosophy and theology occur. What I want to claim is this: the *Iliad* and the *Odyssey* provide us with two competing conceptions of the good and how it is obtained. It is these competing views that prefigure the elaborate metaphysical positions of Plato and Aristotle and subsequently Western Christianity's views on the sacraments. Christians, like the culture around them, must come to terms with food. I am arguing that the dispute over food between Achilles and Odysseus frames and prefigures the debates that Plato and Aristotle would work out. Food, once again, is at the heart of our view of the world.

In book 19 of the *Iliad*, we find Achilles enraged by the death of his friend Patroclus, who was killed by the Trojan hero Hector. Achilles rallies the troops for an assault on the Trojans when a dispute breaks out. The argument between Odysseus and Achilles is essentially over whether lunch would be a good idea at this point. Achilles will have nothing to do with lingering, whereas Odysseus thinks that lunch would be in order. Here is their exchange (Fagles trans.):

> Achilles:
> It's wrong to malinger here with talk, wasting time—
> our great work lies all before us, still to do.
>
> Odysseus:
> Not so quickly, brave as you are, god-like Achilles.
> Achaea's troops are hungry . . .
> No, command them now to take their food and wine
> by the fast ships—a soldier's strength and nerve.
> No fighter can battle all day long, cut and thrust
> till the sun goes down, if he is starved for food.
> Even though his courage may blaze up for combat,
> his limbs will turn to lead before he knows it,
> thirst and hunger will overtake him quickly,
> his knees will cave in as the man struggles on.
> But the one who takes his fill of food and wine
> before he grapples enemies full force, dawn to dusk—
> the heart in his chest keeps pounding fresh with courage,
> nor do his legs give out till all break off from battle.
> Come, dismiss your ranks, have them make their meal.
>
> Achilles:
> You talk of food?
> I have no taste for food—what I really crave
> is slaughter and blood and the choking groans of men!
>
> Odysseus:
> . . . Greater than I, stronger with spears by no small edge—
> yet, I might just surpass you in seasoned judgment
> by quite a lot, since I have years on you
> and I know the world much better . . .

So let your heart be swayed by what I say.
Now fighting men will sicken of battle quickly:
the more dead husks the bronze strews on the ground
the sparser the harvest then, when Zeus almighty
tips his scales and the tide of battle turns—
the great steward on high who rules our mortal wars. (19.190–268)[2]

It is a simple dispute but its metaphysical implications are vast, for it reveals the fundamental orientation toward the world that each hero takes. Achilles, true to form, is ready to disregard the fundamental needs of the body in his pursuit for a disembodied and eternal glory (*kleos*). Odysseus, on the other hand, makes food and the orientation toward the goods of this world a big deal.

Two points regarding Odysseus and food are relevant here. First, Odysseus has a reputation for thinking that meals are important. A few lines before the dispute cited above, Agamemnon chides Odysseus for failing to show the same zeal for battle as he does for a good meal:

Agamemnon (to Odysseus):
First you are, when you hear of feasts from me,
when Achaeans set out banquets for the chiefs.
Then you are happy enough to down the roast meats
and cups of honeyed, mellow wine—all you can drink.
But now you'd gladly watch ten troops of Achaeans
beat you to this feast,
first to fight with the ruthless bronze before you.

Food is a big deal to Odysseus: to be dressed down for thinking too much about his belly and then turn around and argue with Achilles that lunch should be served is no small matter. Second, Odysseus makes the following subtle argument in his exchange with Achilles: we need food because we become food for the gods (Christianity happily reverses this notion with God becoming food for us). The boys should have lunch before battle because warfare is connected to eating, as slain warriors become "husks" cut down by the bronze for the "harvest." Zeus is even compared to a "steward" who presides over this surreal banquet. In denying the importance of food, one attempts to surpass even the gods, for even they are concerned about food and the protocols surrounding it. Food has not only pragmatic significance, but also divine significance for Odysseus.

2. Robert Fagles, trans., *The Iliad* (New York: Viking, 1990).

Why is this dispute really that important? For starters, it frames the important themes of both the *Iliad* and the *Odyssey*. Achilles is, of course, the central focus of the *Iliad*, whereas the *Odyssey* revolves around the character of Odysseus. The *Iliad* is about Achilles's quest for eternal *kleos* or glory, whereas the *Odyssey* can be read as a critique of what Achilles had to do to achieve that kleos: Achilles chooses to die gloriously, never returning home, while Odysseus's tale is all about returning home. Achilles chooses the eternal transcendence of undying fame; Odysseus chooses the immanence of his wife, son, and land. Metaphysically speaking, then, Achilles in the *Iliad* has more in common with Plato than Aristotle. He finds the metaphysical location of the goods he desires not in the contingent things surrounding him, but in the attainment of a transcendent fame that outlasts and supersedes the world of the senses. On the other hand, Odysseus seems to have more in common with Aristotle's metaphysical preference and makes his case not through philosophical argumentation but through his choice to return to those physical things that constitute his world. It would seem that for Achilles the world of the senses is devoid of ultimate meaning and he/we cannot bear it, whereas for Odysseus the world of the senses is where this meaning is ultimately to be found: the physical provides the means of accessing the divine.

TRUE FOOD, TRUE PHYSIS

Food is a big deal. At the advent of Western thought we find a couple of guys disagreeing about when to have lunch, and if I am right, then perhaps this Homeric dispute escalated into one of the most important metaphysical disputes in the history of Greek philosophy. Jesus himself is often in hot water over his relationship to food—for being a glutton, for being an ascetic, for dining with the wrong crowd, and for dining without the concern for the proper religious etiquette.[3]

How do we as Christians fare regarding our orientation toward food and particularly our view of the elements of the table? Following the lead of Achilles, Odysseus, Plato, and Aristotle, we either push for transcendence or immanence. Here is one way of seeing it: Homer needed two epics to fully capture the human experience and its relationship to kleos—the transcendence of Achilles in the *Iliad* and the immanence of Odysseus in the *Odyssey*. Following suit, Achilles-like Plato exhorts us to move beyond the material by organizing our souls in such a way that the appetitive, spirited, and reflective aspects of our persons become entirely oriented to the

3. I would like to thank my colleague Michael Robbins for this observation.

transcendent good that illumines all things, just as the sun makes all things visible. Aristotle, picking up where Odysseus leaves off, exhorts his students to the "this-worldly" study of biology echoing Heraclitus's dictum that "there are gods here, too" (*Parts of Animals* 1.1). The dominant theological paradigms of the West transmitted through the likes of Augustine and Aquinas utilize the good work done by the students of Socrates and formulate the physis of divine food in nearly the same terms: Protestants, Plato-like and pointing skyward, locate the goods beyond the veil of time. Catholics, Aristotle-like, hold fast to the immanent divinity mysteriously present when dinner is served; God is, indeed, here too.

Holding the middle ground is the Bread of Life. It seems fair to say that Christ had the right relationship to food, that he understood its true physis. He knew the importance of dining appropriately: where, when, and with whom. We, on the other hand, at least with respect to our most important meal, have difficulty coming to terms with its physis. We swing from extreme to extreme, unable to hold with the Logos. That this is so should teach us humility regarding the limitations of our religious traditions to get every detail right consistently and should drive us toward an analysis of the worldviews that we appropriate without reflection. Most importantly, it should drive us to the one who eats right and is true physis.

17 The Possibility of an Evangelical Poet

by RYAN HARPER

I AM NOT CERTAIN: WHAT does *evangelical Christian* mean anymore? I see narrow orders, but any tight definition is limited, fraught with complications. I have met self-identified evangelicals who diverge widely in their Christologies and in their approaches to the Bible. I have met Christians who, by any number of doctrinal criteria, might be called *evangelical* but who do not self-identify as such.

Despite my uncertainty about the specifics, I believe *evangelical* still means . . . something. As I scroll back through my encounters with Christians who I feel justified in calling *evangelical* and with Christians who call themselves evangelicals, I am inclined to roll up this sum according to a shared disposition, to a common orientation to the world and its putative creator, rather than according to a circumscribed hermeneutics or soteriology.

In lieu of a tight definition, I offer a general observation: all evangelicals I have ever met want me to *get it*—passionately, thoroughly. Like their universe, they have purpose, and within this purpose is a desire for me to understand the purpose of my (*the*) universe, which is essential, they believe, to my understanding of my own purpose. The pieces of this universe may be multifarious and confounding, but they all fit. In the evangelical view, things resolve—ultimately. There are answers. There is *an* answer, and the answer has something to do with Jesus. It is evangelicals' commission to bear witness to whatever fragments of this answer have been entrusted to them.

Because they take this commission seriously, evangelicals are charged with resolve. Therefore, it is not surprising to find the teleological arc of the universe recapitulated in miniature in evangelical discursive moments. If one knows something about the resolution of the grand narrative—and believes the resolution to provide the key to the rest of the story, the rest of the ostensibly trivial matters, for all of us—one cannot in good faith withhold information when one communicates to others. Whether the good news is "love wins" or "gays lose," the messenger has a teleological imperative to deliver it. My spouse and I often joke about how every Sunday is Easter Sunday in evangelical churches. Go to any evangelical worship service, on any given Sunday, and witness the brilliant acrobatics of a worship team that, absent a Mass and (usually) a liturgical calendar, starts you off at Moses, Job, or Kevin Bacon and deposits you in fewer than six degrees at the cross and then the empty tomb—the sites where, for evangelicals, it is finished. This is what it means to be "purpose driven."

To be sure, many of us are similarly driven—fancying ourselves faithfully completing some good work in others, preaching our own gospels unto someone else's transformation. In this light, evangelicals are a people set apart only by the content of their message. But the content of their message weighs especially heavily on evangelicals for two reasons. First, evangelicals tend to believe in the universal relevance of their specific beliefs. To believe in your own personal Jesus, to believe that he who is Truth for you in your private heart is true for all humans—that is evangelicalism. Second, evangelicals inhabit communities where the most meaningful acts of expression are literal articulations of one's specific core beliefs; for what else really matters but preaching Jesus Christ and him crucified? Because there is too much at stake to leave things hanging, the quality of the articulations resides largely in their logical precision, conciseness, and clarity. Bearing witness means baring meaning. Looser, more suggestive language is at best a means to an end, at worst an unholy distraction. When evangelicals "go, therefore, and make disciples of all nations," their yes should be yes, and their no should be no.

If I am correct about the centrality of a strong teleological imperative to evangelical identity, I wonder about the possibilities of an evangelical poet. Do the mechanics of evangelicalism cut against the grain of the poetic enterprise? In part, I think so. But friction is not simply a wearing away. It may be that, if an evangelical poet is possible, evangelical and literary worlds would grow flush with mutual resistance.

⸺

As most people understand them, poems are texts. When some body of interpretive authorities marks some textual event as a poem, this cues people to become responders of a certain variety. We readers of poems attend to different features in the textual event than we would if we were reading, say, a grocery list or birth announcement. Of course, the criteria and expectations vary. Our best avant-garde poets have made a tradition of unsettling a criterion the moment two or more critics gather to enshrine it, but even the most avant-garde poets know they'll not likely find many of their volumes in the photography section of the bookstore. If they desire a teaching job in something called an English department, they will be glad of this.

Outside of the sublime avant-garde circles in which margins become centers, the fact that poems are texts produces the widespread expectation that poetic language should operate *roughly* like other texts. When most of us read most poems, we expect at the very least moments of coherence and intelligible syntax—some sense that the poet desires to meet us on a common linguistic territory. We come to the poem believing that someone is trying to communicate *with* us. The poem-as-textual-event does not reduce to a poet's unilinear addressing of an audience. Rather, the poem is a genesis pool, a site where meanings are created, contested, and collapsed. Although poets must issue calls, they also must invite responses, responses that, along with the ostensibly original call, co-constitute the poem as event, as art. Even if we allow provisionally that poets are prime movers in the poetic enterprise, poets require partners to create poetry.

Thus construed, poetry poses problems for evangelical communities for whom effective communication occurs more unilinearly—for whom, in the most ideal circumstances, speaker and listener, writer and reader, are fastened ineluctably into an epistemological hierarchy. Evangelical speakers and writers—they are the holders of truths in this hierarchy. It is their charge to dispense these truths to those who have ears to hear.

In such a hierarchy, one might expect the hearers to bear the greater condemnation for communication breakdowns; the hearers are relatively passive, so they are counted as worse than ignorant if they cannot complete so simple a task as to allow the truths to enter them. However, the holders of truths bear the greater burden. They imagine themselves to be elected carriers of the truths, rather than creators or co-creators of truths. Because the truths are considered objective, not quite their own—they do not speak as ones possessing authority, but as guardians of their master's property—they are terrified of misrepresenting, misspeaking, and miswriting, for they know their master to be harsh ("if anyone causes one of these little ones to stumble . . ."). Their terror is compounded by the fact that they imagine their audience to be sheep easily led astray. Complicating and further exacerbating their anxiety is the reality that in Protestant America—where all believers speak as priests, where the customer is always right—the sheep feel entitled to hold the shepherd accountable, by any number of shifting standards. And the sheep can be harsh masters. Therefore, the transmitters of truths must execute their textual duties in as unadorned fashion as possible. Narrow and straight. No room for metaphor, mystery, audience (mis)interpretation, let alone co-creation. As a result, the textual events that evangelicals value tend to manifest a nervous hermeneutical hording of the author to himself—a passionate guarding of the terms, supposedly undertaken for the sake of the gospel and for the sake of the sheep.

How suspicious Louise Glück's conceptualizing of poetry would sound to the would-be evangelical poet:

> At the heart of [the poem] will be a question, a problem. And we will feel, as we read, a sense that the poet was not wed to any one outcome. The poems themselves are like experiments, which the reader is freely invited to recreate in his own mind. Those poets who claustrophobically oversee or bully or dictate response prematurely advertise the deficiencies of the chosen particulars, as though without strenuous guidance the reader might not reach an intended conclusion. Such work suffers from the excision of doubt; Milton may have written proofs, but his poems compel because they dramatize questions. The only illuminations are like Psyche's, who did not know what she'd find.[1]

Glück presents a paradoxical poetic imperative: effective poets wed themselves to nonweddedness. Poets should bring no obvious finality of vision to bear on their poems, but display themselves as open to contingency. Abandoning "proofs," poets provide in their poems no more than an arrangement of items that may or may not provoke readers to the conclusions the poets had in mind when they wrote or released the poems into the world.

Any shrewd evangelical will immediately recognize that this noncommittedness is a sort of commitment—one that bespeaks a particular orientation to one's self and one's environment, not simply a literary methodology. It requires a poet to possess faith in the necessity and capability of readers. It demands that a poet place greater value on the process of illumination that the poem puts into motion than on the poet's particular illuminations regarding the world. It asks a poet to produce, first and foremost, possibility—not consensus, not resolutions.

1. Louise Glück, "Against Sincerity," in *Proofs and Theories: Essays on Poetry* (Hopewell, NJ: Ecco, 1994) 45.

Is it possible for evangelicals to commit to such noncommittedness and remain committed evangelicals, or do poets operate based on a competing, irreconcilable worldview? If evangelicals are as I have described them, I fear the latter is true.

But surely evangelical Christianity houses more tenets than a rigorous teleology and a tightly ordered communicative theory. Evangelicals claim to follow a teacher who described the kingdom of God in parables, who came to call his disciples not servants but friends. Perhaps contingency, uncertainty, and open-ended dialogue with readers are not as inimical to evangelicalism as it seems on first blush.

It may be that evangelicals who dedicate themselves to poetry will come to (re)learn through poetry that commitment to contingency is continuous with their faith—perhaps a centerpiece of their faith. If one key component of Christianity is the recognition of all humans' creatureliness—that is, recognition of our relative finitude, our non-Godness, our mutability, our transformability, and our perpetual need for transformation and grace—should not an acknowledgement of one's own creatureliness require a faithful embrace of contingency? If evangelicals believe one of the two greatest commandments is to love their neighbors as themselves, what else does this mean but to open themselves to possible transformation through encounters with others, the very sorts of transformation that evangelicals expect others to be open to when evangelicals express their own proofs and theories? Can evangelical faith really thrive under the denial of risk, the excision of doubt?

If the poetic enterprise offers a challenge to the tight circumscriptions of purpose-driven evangelicalism, it also reminds evangelicals of the more unwieldy, elusive blossoms that spring perennially, if sporadically, in their own garden. I subscribe to a Christian literary magazine whose subtitle is "Art. Faith. Mystery." The possibility of the evangelical poet may depend upon evangelicals conceiving of the members of this trinity as consubstantial.

⸻

Louise Glück's call for poets to embrace open-endedness are not new. She writes in the spirit of the great American poets of contingency—Walt Whitman, Charles Olson, and A. R. Ammons, to name a few. Although this tradition resonates with me, historically it has a troubling upshot.

Demands for open-endedness often become entangled with endorsements of dogmatic disinterestedness—the sorts of which the New Critics and mid-century moderns like Anthony Hecht celebrated—for example, in this, Hecht's paraphrase of W. H. Auden:

> If some person came to [Auden] and said, "I want to be a poet because
> I have something very urgent and important to express," chances are,
> he or she would not be a poet. But if they said instead, "I am inter-
> ested in putting words together in novel and unexpected ways. I like
> playing with words, with language." This is someone who might very
> well turn out to be a poet.[2]

So the argument goes; the formalistic craft of poetry must be the compositional prime mover. The poet must distance herself from the concerns of the world and its citizens, all for the sake of the craft. Or the poet can care about the things of the world; those cares just cannot drive the poetic enterprise—the assumption being that poets driven by any righteous cause other than the cause of righteous craft quickly become crude pamphleteers, pontificating prosaically about the plight of the poor, the sexually marginal, the cultural outsider. Furthermore, because the power of the righteous cause—or the power of the poet's conviction—will not suffice to render a powerful poem, the righteous-cause poet damages both the formalistic quality *and* the prophetic witness of the poem. Therefore, the righteous-cause poet ultimately nullifies her ultimate concern.

Be they pietistic or Marxist, righteous causes certainly have fueled a lot of bad poetry. And if it is legitimate to believe Hecht composed "More Light! More Light!" in a mood of calculated disinterestedness, there is indeed an explosive and chilling pathos—a cold fusion—to a disinterested approach.[3]

But pure disinterestedness is impossible. I believe most poets accept this impossibility intellectually. Most of us in the humanities, having imbued Michel Foucault, if not Friedrich Nietzsche, likely will nod lazily when someone claims that *some* interest undergirds all of our endeavors. The impossibility of disinterestedness becomes especially clear in retrospect; one need not be a brilliant theorist of race or gender to note the very particular interests attached to the New Critical proclamations of disinterestedness.

But practically, in our own moment of creation, contemporary poets frequently take on the New Critical mantra, denying that interests substantially inform their craft. This is especially true and especially troubling in a generation in which poetry has become specialized and professionalized to an unprecedented degree. Poets literally cannot afford to think that their creative writing programs have interests other

2. Quoted in *The Poet's View*, directed by Mel Stuart (New York: Academy of American Poets, 1993).

3. See Anthony Hecht, "More Light! More Light!," in *Collected Earlier Poems: The Complete Texts of The Hard Hours, Millions of Strangers, The Venetian Vespers* (New York: Knopf, 1990).

than shaping them into good craftspeople—or that the very notion of a professional craft is politicized, predicated upon the exclusion of voices that are "interested" in toppling one of the craft's current load-bearing pillars. Academic poets (and, in a sense, that includes all of us who attempt to publish in the epoch of academic professionalism) cannot afford to think that the academy teaches unto its own perpetuity, rewards only usable or ignorable dynamisms, and restricts those experiments of form and content that would shake foundations. We of the academy cannot afford to think that our institutions' interests have any meaningful effect on what we write, how we write, or the fact *that* we write. When we narrate ourselves to ourselves and others, either we must employ that tired old romance of the academic visionary versus the academic moneymen—in which singular professors or perhaps their departments practice their genius surreptitiously, away from the watchful eyes of the cold pragmatists in the administrative building whose vision extends only to the financial bottom line—or we must imagine that the academy, like us, possesses a disinterested singularity that allows for the flourishing of our disinterested singularity. There are manifold career incentives simply to take our stipends and salaries and to proclaim ourselves free artists, open to contingency, working in a free space, alongside people who are open to whatever our disinterested jaunts into the unknown yield. I write presently in one of the historic stone structures of Princeton University. It is silent and windless here; untroubled, a writer could draft and draft. The very stones cry out on my behalf.

When I read some of the tunnel-vision academic poetry of the twenty-first century, I cannot believe this species of disinterestedness is desirable. By "tunnel-vision" I do not mean simply autobiographical poetry, for it requires wide eyes to see oneself. Rather, I mean poetry that fancies the world—including potential readers—as being thoroughly external to the poet and merely incidental to the poem. This is a sign of disinterestedness-turned-disconnectedness, which is a predictable but unfortunate perversion of that disinterestedness which attempts to meet the world on the world's terms, to hand some of the meaning making over to the reader, to transform the poetic enterprise into communion. The disconnected poet has no true community—for true communities house substantive dissenters. The disconnected poet answers to no one but species of himself—or to the program that created him, which is usually nothing more than his own ego writ large. Such a poet becomes a soliloquist—and not a very good one, because good soliloquists have seen the world, have listened in terrible wonder as their voices bend back to them from the backs of theaters, have seen the shadow their bodies cast on the stage floor, dark and un-steady. The disconnected poet conceives neither of the world nor of himself in it.

Because he mistakes indifference toward the tension and conflict inherent in a radically open-ended universe for a strenuous inhabiting of the tension and conflict, the disconnected poet presumptuously delights in his own negative capability. He believes he has accepted a Keatsian uncertainty, a comfort with the absence of reso-lution, when in fact he merely has exempted himself from involvement with and re-sponsibility to the world, its citizens, and the contingencies that go with them. When the disconnected poet dramatizes questions—not realizing that the dramatization of particular questions as opposed to other questions reveals particular commit-ments on his part—he is guarding his singularity by exonerating himself from his-tory, which perpetually requires humans to provide answers, however provisional. This sort of poet is every bit as condescending and feckless as the poet who bullies an intended response from readers. The Great Dramatizer of Questions is beyond challenge. It takes no great courage to invite readers to respond to one's questions, for questions are designed for responses. It takes some courage, some risking of the self, to invite readers to respond to one's answers.

Enter the evangelical, who has the audacity to wear her commitments in the public square. No doubt, many of her commitments might strike nonevangelicals as parochial. But only a cosmopolitan of the most parochial variety would view a person's parochialisms as reason enough to scoff at all of her particularities. Only a pluralist of the narrowest sort would refuse to countenance the widely resonant commitments an evangelical voices as a consequence of her particular theological commitments. We all may not be able to gleefully recite John 3:16 in the same spirit as an evangelical, but we may recognize, respect, and even learn from a person who takes God's love for the world to mean she must commit herself to resist oppression, renounce violence, and prioritize the experiences of the marginalized. True, these are not the only commitments various evangelicals might regard as commensurable with their theologies, as the all-too-frequent alignment of American evangelicalism with American imperialism resoundingly demonstrates. But the legacy of resistance is still there among evangelicals. The tradition of giving voice to the voiceless is still there. Especially (but not exclusively) among young evangelicals today, an increas-ingly vocal impatience abounds with a Christianity that serves as ornamentation for the rich and powerful. Many of these voices presently may be sighs too deep for words. But they will become words in time, if these evangelicals find a community where prophets are not without honor.

Such evangelicals more nearly approximate the prophetic valence of poetry—especially American poetry—than do those whose celebrations of disinterestedness blind them to the very imminent disasters to which a non-circumspect disinterestedness can lead. For surely the poetic enterprise is built on more than a foundational commitment to noncommitment. Many of the great poets wrote as particularly committed people. This is true even of the great poets of contingency. Walt Whitman was driven both by the (re)vision of his craft and by his democratic vistas; the two drives mutually informed one another. It was not simply the search for new aesthetic forms that caused Adrienne Rich to chart a path from Rukeyser, to dive into the wreck of patriarchy; it was not simply novel wordplay with which Rich surfaced—transformed, a radically new radical poet. Even William Carlos Williams—one of Glück's outcome-disregarding lodestars—had something generally democratic in mind when he made a start out of particulars; something gave him the idea to turn from ideas, toward the things themselves. Scope eluded Ammons's grasp, but he still allowed himself eddies of meaning: those eddies always swirled around Ammons's commitment to the individual soul's inviolable capacity for radiance. A directed contingency—a mobile and powerful telos, a heated fission—charged all of these poets. They wrote poetry out of and unto a vision of how the world was and might be. Were this not the case, we would not be drawn to their radiance. We might pick up their volumes once; we would not pick them up twice.

Evangelical commitment does not merely translate to exhortation. It also often results in profound self-examination. The pixilated, round-the-clock bombast of jeremiadists often overshadows this characteristic of evangelicalism, but it is a serious facet of evangelical piety. Evangelicals are compelled to understand their own brokenness, their own complicity in the wrongs they perceive in the "external" world, their own need for redemption, their own potential for offering redemption. True, there are evangelicals who either do little self-examination or who predicate their examination upon fraudulent dichotomies; evangelical soul-searching can become a Manichean project of escape from either the material world or society or both—a simple matter of figuring out how to be "in the world but not of it," how to hole up like the great Carmelite poet, recusing oneself alone from involvement in the hellish world of other people. But I do not find, on the whole, that evangelicals are prone to unaffected removal from the world. Their world-loving God calls loudly. Especially among Reformed evangelicals who claim the likes of Jonathan Edwards as their theo-cultural heritage, I find a great deal of intense, honest, and communal introspection—a passionate and persistent ambivalence toward the self that is of a piece with their passionate and persistent ambivalence toward their world. If through their self-examination evangelicals maintain hope for personal transformation (without which there is mute despair) and hope for the world's transformation (without which there is self-righteous apathy), the ambivalence is productive: the beginning of all transformations.

I return to Glück, this time on the poet's motivation and mood: "When the force and misery of compulsion are missing, when the scar is missing; the ambivalence which seeks, in the self, responsibility . . . when ambivalence toward the self is missing, the written recreation, no matter how artful, forfeits emotional authority."[4] I believe evangelicals might be predisposed uniquely toward these blessings and curses of temperament. It makes many of them anxious, somewhat neurotic people (hardly a disqualifier for membership in poetry guilds). It is hard to imagine a literary community that would not benefit from having such tormented, loving people of faith as fellow citizens. We need writers so passionately committed, writers who have something urgent and important to communicate. The world groans for their transformation.

4. Glück, "The Forbidden," in *Proofs and Theories*, 54.

18 Faithful to the Work: An Interview with John Leax

by DANIEL BOWMAN JR.

A N ELDER STATESMAN IN art and faith circles, John Leax (Jack to friends) is a poet and essayist of hard-earned, humble wisdom, and as such, he avoids the spotlight. The author of books like *Country Labors: Poems for All Seasons* and *Out Walking: Reflections on Our Place in the Natural World*, he would rather be working in the garden than at the podium, and since retiring from a long teaching career at Houghton College, Jack has done just that. But he has also been busy putting the finishing touches on three forthcoming books. In this interview, Leax discusses his early days as a poet of faith, his adoption of Wendell Berry's metaphor of "at-one-ment" in his life and writing, his efforts to break with the confessional voice, and the process of compiling his new books.

The Other Journal (TOJ): In 2009, you retired after more than forty years of teaching. What have you been up to since then?

John Leax (JL): The first thing I did, after redesigning my garden and making some sculptures for it, was read William Wordsworth's *The Prelude* and Dorothy Wordsworth's journals. Those, along with my daily work in the garden, turned me back to Alexander Pope. I wintered with him and a stack of books about his gardening. During Lent, I gave myself up to Milton—*Paradise Lost* and *Paradise Regained*. Pope and Milton sent me to the Latin poets. I read all of Virgil, and then Ovid's *Metamorphoses*, which I had only dipped into in the past. It was exciting to discover it as a single, whole poem. From there I moved on to Horace's *Odes*.

The garden and pastoral themes in all of that reading led me into the Italian Renaissance, to Petrarch, Boccaccio, and Dante. My next reading project is Spenser's *The Faerie Queene*. I'm anxious to see how I get on with that. As I was taking in all this foundational Western stuff, I was also working through David Hinton's translations of Chinese "river and mountain poets," roughly the fifth through the thirteenth century. And underlining all of this was a body of devotional reading: the desert fathers and mothers, selections from *Philokalia*, Eusebius, *Early Christian Lives* by Athanasius and Jerome, and Augustine's *City of God*.

Recounting my reading this way sounds so pretentious that it scares me. I guess that after all those years of teaching the twentieth century, I'm running to the sources as fast as I can. Needless to say, this is forcing me to rethink and revise my current writing projects.

The first writing project, a selection of poems from the last twenty years, is more or less finished. I'm calling it *Recluse Freedom: Poems 1990–2010*. WordFarm has it scheduled for publication in 2012. The second is a collection of sonnets on biblical themes that is about two-thirds done. And third is a collaborative project with Jeanne Murray Walker and Robert Siegel, a collection of epistolary poems on the seven deadly sins. We've been working on it for more years than there are sins; I've no idea when we'll finish.

TOJ: In the literary nonfiction course I've taught at Houghton, we've studied books by Gregory Wolfe, Alan Jacobs, Andy Crouch, Marilyn McEntyre, and others, as well as *A Syllable of Water: Twenty Writers of Faith Reflect on Their Art* and *Shouts and Whispers: Twenty-One Writers Speak about Their Writing and Their Faith*—a collection of transcribed talks from Calvin College's Festival of Faith and Writing. We've also looked at pieces from *Image, Books and Culture*, and *The Other Journal*.

All this to say that today's writing students at Christian colleges are growing up in an environment rich with contemporary material that examines the relationship between faith and serious literary writing. I know it wasn't always so.

Could you take us back to a time before this proliferation, in the early part of your career? What did the art-and-faith writing landscape look like when you were starting out?

JL: This is a harder question to address than it appears because, I think, the answer must be fairly personal, even granting that the personal is experienced within the larger cultural atmosphere.

I remember a series of contradictions. I studied, during my prep school years at the Stony Brook School, with Frank Gaebelein. A superb biblical scholar, he was also a man of sophisticated taste in the arts—he was a pianist, a writer, and also a mountain climber; he encouraged his students to be involved in culture, to understand, to be creative. He represented everything I still find most positive about an integrated life of faith and art.

On the other hand, much of what I encountered could be summarized in this story: midway through my junior year of college, I dropped out and worked as a laborer for a year. Just before returning to school, I had an interview with the senior pastor of the large, downtown Presbyterian church I attended. This was not a fundamentalist church. After a long discussion about getting my life in order, I finally asked him what he thought of the poems that I had given him. His response was brutal: "It's time to put that nonsense aside, young man, and get to work."

Two books helped me. One was Henry Zylstra's *Testament of Vision*. The other, the more important one, was a little Pendle Hill Pamphlet by the Quaker artist Fritz Eichenberg, *Art and Faith*. From that I took two principles. The first I can quote: "Speed is the enemy of the craftsman." The second is that one must step aside from economic ambitions or ambitions of success to be faithful to the work. These books allowed me to believe not only that a life of poetry was possible, but also that it was good.[1]

I went to Wheaton, and while at Wheaton I encountered for the first time the world of the fundamentalist. Wheaton in the early sixties was an exciting place: full of controversy and discussion about the arts. Students were trying to break free from the fundamentalism, but I found the atmosphere oppressive. There was a very strong ethical perspective on the arts; you had to be careful of the arts because they would lead people astray. It was your responsibility as the artist to anticipate what somebody might do with your words or images, so you simply could not take any kind of risk.

There is, I'm sure, something to be said for that ethical concern, and I'm glad I've been affected by my exposure to it, but at the same time, it is a limiting and ultimately deadening approach. It makes the weakest person—the person most easily offended or most willing to be offended—the arbiter of the culture. I don't think we can allow that to define us. We do have a responsibility to our brothers and sisters, but if we have vocations as artists, we also have a responsibility to the work, and that's what was not understood.

1. See Henry Zylstra, *Testament of Vision* (Grand Rapids: Eerdmans: 1967); and Fritz Eichenberg, *Art and Faith*, Pendle Hill Pamphlet 68 (Wallingford, PA: Pendle Hill, 1952).

TOJ: Let me follow up on the topic of models. Many of us now can look to contemporary artists of faith who are producing work of high literary quality. What poets and writers of faith did you look to as models when you first started out?

JL: Very few, very few. In my college years I had C. S. Lewis and Thomas Merton. They were the only figures of any stature I was aware of. When I started writing poems my senior year of high school, I was influenced by Robert Lowell and Allen Ginsberg. This was shortly after Lowell had published his *Life Studies*, so it was not the Catholic Lowell of the early books—the elaborate and technical Lowell—it was the Lowell breaking loose into confessional verse. And of course Ginsberg was largely confessional in his work.

The one poet I did meet at Wheaton was Chad Walsh, one of the founders of the *Beloit Poetry Journal*. He was an Episcopal priest. And over the years he was personally very encouraging to me. But I don't think his verse influenced me. What he gave me was permission to be a poet. His suggestion that if one is a Christian and one is a poet, one can't help but be a Christian poet, was very helpful to me at that time. It kept me a bit looser about the subject than some of my friends.

But other models—there really weren't many. I was looking to secular poets. Merton didn't become the crucial influence he has been until I rediscovered him in my early thirties.

TOJ: How did you begin building community with other literary poets of faith?

JL: At Wheaton, Jeanne Murray Walker was a good friend. We made great progress as poets in the back row of a physical geology class, where we mostly wrote poems and critiqued each other's work while the world of "Rocks for Jocks" swirled around us. I think I was somewhat in awe of her work then, and I still am.

I traveled pretty much alone for quite a while. I left Wheaton, finished at Houghton, and went on to Johns Hopkins, where I worked with Elliott Coleman, another Episcopal poet. When I came to Houghton to teach, Lionel Basney and I started a little magazine of our own (*Ktaadn*). This was in the era where everybody who wanted to be a poet started a magazine. We even learned to do letterpress printing. I think I would be an entirely different and lesser poet and person apart from my friendship and twenty-five years of collaboration with Lionel. Though he never published a book of poems, he was the better craftsman.

The little magazine allowed us to begin making connections. One day we got a letter and a stack of poems from this person who wrote, "I'm a friend of Jeanne Walker, and she said I should send you some stuff." So Lionel and I took a look at the poems and said, "Well, this has some promise." Full of the arrogance forgivable only in the young still defining themselves, we sent it back and said, "If you make these changes, we'll use it." And the writer, with what I have learned is the spirit that characterizes her passionate desire to learn to be a better poet and to seek greater excellence, agreed to the changes. That exchange began a long friendship with Luci Shaw.

Working on *Ktaadn* allowed us to establish this circle that continued to expand, because as you met one poet, he or she disclosed another. We corresponded with and published early work by Leslie Leyland Fields, Diane Glancy, Jean Janzen, James Schaap, Hugh Cook, and others. We were also able to work with established poets like Samuel Hazo, a Catholic poet from Pittsburgh; John Bennett, who was also one of the founders of the *Beloit Poetry Journal*; and Arnold Kenseth, a wonderful poet we met through Chad Walsh. Kenseth spent his life as a Congregational pastor in New England all the while writing superb poems, including a delightful book called *The Holy Merriment*. He's a George Herbert for the twentieth century, but hardly anybody knows him.[2] A truly great figure we were able to publish and who I eventually met on a couple occasions was Thomas Merton's friend Robert Lax. Lax was from down the road in Olean, New York, though he was living on Patmos in Greece when we corresponded with him.

We were blessed.

TOJ: The dedication of your collection *Country Labors*, to your wife, begins, "Hands worn hard by labor give / better tongue to truth than words." And the poem "Here" from that collection includes the lines, ". . . and we, faithful, bound / flesh to flesh learn / in brokenness the changes / loves works in fertile soil." I'm interested in the relationship between these two strands in your life and your poetics: working the earth and writing.[3]

JL: I think that to answer this question I need to talk about metaphor. In his essay "Discipline and Hope," Wendell Berry writes about the "at-one-ment" metaphor: the farmer and his field, the marriage of the husband and wife, the spiritual relationship of Creator and creation—he points out that each of these is a metaphor of the others so that they all interconnect.[4] We understand our relation to the creation as we

---

2. See Arnold Kenseth, *The Holy Merriment*, Contemporary Poets Series (Chapel Hill: University of North Carolina Press, 1963).

3. John Leax, *Country Labors: Poems for All Seasons* (Grand Rapids: Zondervan, 1991).

4. Wendell Berry, *A Continuous Harmony: Essays Cultural and Agricultural* (New York: Harcourt Brace Jovanovich).

understand our relationship to other people (the marriage relationship standing in for the social). We understand God as we understand people as we understand creation. Should any one of those metaphors be broken, our ability to understand the others is going to be limited.

So the metaphor has a direct correspondence to our ability to function in reality. When I wrote *In Season and Out*, I engaged in a very deliberate exploration of that metaphor. I set out to write every day for a year looking for these intersections, to see if, in fact, this was an accurate description of the world. I found it accurate. Perhaps more importantly, writing the book caused me to *enact* that metaphor. Being conscious of looking for it, I was also creating it. And I think that's part of what happens. As C. S. Lewis says that "Myth becomes fact," I would say that metaphor becomes fact, that this exploration of metaphor requires wholeness in one's work so that one *must* engage the physical world in order to be a poet. They interact, interlock; one leads to the other. Putting that metaphor at the center of *In Season and Out*, and consequently everything I've done since, has set up that relationship, the terms of my *being here*.[5]

TOJ: Speaking of "here," you're known as a writer of place, and you are often called upon to reflect on what that means. In an essay in *A Syllable of Water*, you note that all you have to say about place grows from the central metaphor of your life, which is being in Christ and that "rather than simplifying anything, having one's place in Christ complicates one's life, for the . . . spiritual ecology is all-inclusive. I am in a place in a process that remains beyond my comprehension." Could you talk a little more about this spiritual ecology?[6]

JL: You can't talk about creation without talking about the Creator. And you can't talk about the Creator without talking about creation. This is the at-one-ment metaphor we've been describing: everything is connected to everything else. You experience both the Creator and the creation in a body in a particular place. There's no other way to experience life and remain human. The body is important; it is our means of apprehension.

If you're going to approach this as a Christian, when you talk about the Creator, you're going to have to talk about the Trinitarian God. It's not just that the Father is

5. See John Leax, *In Season and Out* (Grand Rapids: Zondervan, 1985); and C. S. Lewis, "Myth Becomes Fact," in *God in the Dock: Essays on Theology and Ethics* (Grand Rapids: Eerdmans, 1970).

6. Emilie Griffin, ed., *A Syllable of Water: Twenty Writers of Faith Reflect on Their Art* (Brewster, MA: Paraclete, 2008).

maker, but that the Spirit is present at creation, the Son is present at creation, and creation is not something that happened a long time ago; it's continuing to happen. Your presence in it is part of what it is. By walking through a field, you're making the field a different place. And you, of course, can comprehend it only partially. But any ecology that does not include the intersection of the natural and the supernatural, or the eternal and the temporal, is reductive and incomplete. This apprehension becomes infinitely complicated—and infinitely exciting.

TOJ: Many readers know you best for *Grace Is Where I Live*. How do you account for the popularity of that book?[7]

JL: [*Laughs*] I can't. It puzzles me—though I think its reputation has exceeded its sales! The only suggestion I would make is that it is a collection of pieces that were written over a long period of time. Each essay was written to address some specific question for a particular audience in a particular time. I suspect that particularity may be what explains the immediacy, the concreteness, or whatever it is that people respond to in it. It's a puzzling book for me because it was written over so many years that when I put it together, I felt I was gathering things I had left behind. I'm not sure I know the person who wrote that book anymore.

TOJ: In *Tabloid News*, you take on bizarre premises such as "Smartest Ape in the World Goes to College" and one of my favorites, "Duck Hunters Shoot Angel." How did this come about, in light of your previous work as a poet and essayist?[8]

JL: That's an excellent question to follow what I just said about not knowing the person who wrote *Grace Is Where I Live*. I suspect a reader of *Grace Is Where I Live* wouldn't recognize the author of it as the writer of *Tabloid News*.

In *Grace*, there's a piece called "Sabbatical Journal," in which I wrote about the constraints of the confessional mode. Up through *Country Labors*, when you come across the word "I" in one of my poems, it's me. It's nobody else; it's not a persona. I was trying to tell not only Truth with a capital "T," but also a literal truth: if something is described in the poem, it more or less really happened. I began to find that very constraining. I was becoming increasingly private and reclusive as a person and not wanting to talk about myself. But I didn't know how to change the terms of the

7. See John Leax, *Grace Is Where I Live: Writing as a Christian Vocation* (Grand Rapids: Baker, 1993).

8. John Leax, *Tabloid News: Poems* (La Porte, ID: WordFarm, 2005).

relationship I'd had with my readers. I'd come to the point where I either had to find some way to change or just quit writing poems.

The device of *Tabloid News*, in which there could be no confusion with the events and the characters of the poems with reality, gave me a way to make that break with the confessional voice. It was a turning point. The bizarreness of the situations let me consider and say things that I previously couldn't address or say because of the expectations I'd set up for my audience. So the "Smartest Ape in the World" can say things that the dumbest professor in the world can't!

Nobody's going to confuse the speaker or the characters in the poems with me; that was the key. And this is what's governing the sonnets I'm writing now. Though they're on biblical themes, I'm essentially continuing the same project. Instead of looking at the tabloids in the supermarket, I'm reading and rereading the Gospels and wondering what the person in this or that situation would say. It allows me to explore all these voices and perspectives that the confessional mode didn't allow.

TOJ: I love that you began that departure in the extreme by inhabiting some of the most bizarre voices available.

JL: Well, some of the voices I hear in the Gospels are pretty bizarre, too!

TOJ: The trajectory of your writing career includes several of these departures from the norm—not only in *Tabloid News*, but also with books like *Standing Ground*, which is not simply a collection of essays but an extended record of action and contemplation in light of events that took place in your community. What is the story behind that book?[9]

JL: It's connected again to that metaphor of at-one-ment. What occurred was that in late '89 and early '90, a federal law was passed requiring states to accept ownership of all nuclear waste generated in the state and to provide a place of disposal. New York State decided that they would build a nuclear dump, and the three sites chosen as the finalists in the selection process were all here in Allegany County. People in the community were, of course, disturbed. Everybody from far away, accused the community people of taking a "not in my backyard" stance. There was probably an element of that, but I think there was a larger issue of environmental justice.

There has always been a political element in my work; I think the metaphor of at-one-ment, as innocuous as it sounds, is quite political once you begin to apply it.

9. John Leax, *Standing Ground: A Personal Story of Faith and Environmentalism* (Grand Rapids: Zondervan, 1991).

I'd been doing a lot of writing on creation, on *environmentalism*, for lack of a better term, and I became involved in the expression of concern in the community. Eventually I became an advocate and practitioner of civil disobedience. Though I kept a pair of wooden shoes my father brought back from Europe after WWII on my desk during those days, I never rose to monkey wrenching.

About the same time these events were taking place, the Chrysostom Society, of which I'm a member, contracted to do a book called *Stories for the Christian Year*. Being a perfectly good Protestant with a most superficial understanding of the Christian year, I offered to do Lent. My idea was to journal on the relationship of faith to the creation for the forty days of the season. It turned out that this corresponded to the period of greatest intensity of the nuclear waste protests. I was journaling on it daily. When I was done, I wrote a 5,000-word excerpt from that journal for the Chrysostom book. Virginia Owens read the complete journal and thought it should be a book, and fortunately, Bob Hudson at Zondervan thought so also.

TOJ: That's interesting in terms of shedding light on the role of the writer, in part, as the voice or conscience of the culture.

JL: Perhaps the most moving incident of that time came toward the end of the action. One of the people with whom I had worked said to me, "I envy you. Your faith has given you something I don't have: images and metaphors to talk about these concerns." He also gave me a T-shirt that said, "Nuke a gay baby seal for Jesus."

TOJ: There are several new books on the way. One is your new collection *Recluse Freedom*. What has gone into this collection?

JL: It has twenty years worth of poems in it, more than any other book of mine, so it's diverse. But I think it's an accurate reflection of this whole movement of understanding the spiritual ecology we've been talking about. The opening section is a long poem, "Writing Home." I began it about 1990, and it is part of the most confessional section. But it's moving, formally, into blank verse and into a more abstract way of talking. In it I'm trying to articulate "home" narratively. Then there's a section of prose poems that alternate with very formal, repetitive lyric interludes. I wrote them when I was teaching in the Adirondacks. They're an exploration of being *out* of place while still exploring connections with the world; they're a counter to the first poem. The last section of the book, what I call the Flat Mountain Poems, is the section that excites me most. Flat Mountain is that place where the temporal and the eternal intersect. It's a place that is nowhere and everywhere. The section is a very deliberate exploration of the spiritual ecology, and it is much influenced by the reading of Chinese poets.

So, the book begins in my original voice; the prose poems bring in invention, a little bit of fantasy, and a more varied, less personal voice; and by the time we get to the Flat Mountain Poems, I cannot be trusted. There is a figure in the poems wandering around who has done some of the things I've done and who does things I would like to do; but it's a fictive figure.

TOJ: You also mentioned working on a series of poems on the seven deadly sins written with two other poets. Could you describe the process that you, Jeanne Murray Walker, and Robert Siegel have engaged in collaboratively writing that collection?

JL: This was Bob Siegel's idea. Bob and Jeanne were both at Houghton for the Writing Festival, and while Bob and I were off walking in Letchworth, Bob suggested we write a collaborative poem. We decided that the seven deadly sins would be fun to explore in a series of letters we would write to each other. On the way to the airport, Jeanne and Bob decided that Jeanne should be in on it also. I wrote the first poem to Bob, in which I rambled on in general about sin. He wrote a response to that and sent the two to Jeanne, and she wrote a response to them. Then we launched into the seven particular sins—we've since cut those first three poems, but they were necessary to get into the project.

I see the poem much from the perspective of my reading of Pope: a kind of verse essay, an ability to talk about all sorts of things, to go anywhere. It's kind of a kitchen sink poem—you just toss into it whatever comes into your mind the way you can in a personal essay. They are mostly written in loose blank verse. But how do you hold together a long poem? What formal elements are necessary? As I'm revising it, I'm putting the sections I didn't write in blank verse into blank verse, trying to make it a little more formally unified.

What's curious, of course, is that if one person makes a change, it affects the next person's poem, so I don't know if we'll ever finish it. Maybe it won't be until we're all dead and an editor straightens it out! We keep making changes, then we have to make another change in response, and we're trying to do this on three people's schedules.

It has been very important to me to be involved in this exchange with two poets whom I learn so much from every time I hear from them. Since I'm no longer traveling and getting out like I used to, it's been lifesaving to be involved in this. Working on it has also had a profound effect on my perception and understanding of sin.

TOJ: A recent issue of *Comment* magazine is called *Letters to the Young*. It features a series of essays in which writers, artists, critics, pastors, and others offer wisdom to their counterparts at earlier stages within their respective callings. What would you say in a letter to a young writer of faith?

JL: I'm increasingly reluctant to say much to the young writer. But since you ask, I guess I should venture something. My experience is that faith allowed me to take risks in life and writing that I wouldn't have taken otherwise. It allowed me to live largely outside the core of the literary world and to become a writer I never would have become had I followed the instincts I had during my graduate program and in my early publishing.

It's not an experience that's totally positive; there's a great loneliness to it. But there's something profoundly good about that. It forces one to live in hope, not expectation. It allows one to realize—at least some of the time—that what matters is the work working in you and leading you forward, not the successes, the publications, the prizes, to realize that you, in fact, are part of the work you're writing.

19 Two Poems

by J O H N L E A X

**Walking the Circuit around the Cornfield I Walk Every Day,
I Glimpse the Nature of Creation and Submit to Joy**

Beneath the intermittent buzz of cars
spinning down the two-lane,
of trucks rumbling home,
the constancy of water falling to the river
lives, a rocky song rising
over the silent corn.
In summer air the tassels are still.

Gnats swirl in the sharp light,
a constellation of dark amazements
turning about a moving center.

Though all creation groans,
the movement of the leaves
in the tallest cottonwoods
betrays the presence
of the wind:

the love that calls each moment forth
desires gnats and corn
and walkers blessed with ears and eyes.

*Late Night: Thinking of William Carlos Williams, I Remember
the Red Wheelbarrow and the Old Statue of St. Francis in the Shed*

What does it matter, if I say
this or that—revise my poems,
wheel rocks from the river
to line the dry stream
through the garden,
pull weeds?

I come and go;
it's all the same—
one yielding.

When I mow the lawn,
I pause to urge small toads
from the mower's path.

When I'm awakened by the screech owl's
falling call, I lean out the window,
listen, answer, if necessary
with words.

Contributors

Chris Anderson is Professor of English at Oregon State University. He is also a Catholic deacon. A new book of his poems, *The Next Thing Always Belongs*, will be published this fall by Airlie Press.

Elizabeth L. Antus is a PhD candidate in systematic theology at the University of Notre Dame. Her dissertation will center around the topic of Christian self-love using Augustine of Hippo, Teresa of Ávila, and Sarah Coakley. Her interests include Christian theological anthropology, feminist and womanist theologies, Christian approaches to the question of suffering, disability studies, the TV show *30 Rock*, and her dog, Jubilee.

Daniel Bowman Jr.'s work has appeared in the *Adirondack Review, American Poetry Journal, Cha, Istanbul Literary Review, Midwest Quarterly, Rio Grande Review, Seneca Review*, and many others. A native of upstate New York, he now lives in Indiana where he teaches English at Taylor University.

Peter M. Candler Jr. is Associate Professor of Theology in the Honors College at Baylor University.

William T. Cavanaugh is Senior Research Professor in the Center for World Catholicism and Intercultural Theology at DePaul University. His latest books are *Migrations of the Holy* (2011) and *The Myth of Religious Violence* (2009). His books have been translated into French, Spanish, and Polish.

Matthew Dickerson is the author or coauthor of several books, including *From Homer to Harry Potter: A Handbook of Myth and Fantasy* (2006); *Ents, Elves, and Eriador: The Environmental Vision of J. R. R. Tolkien* (2006); and *Narnia and the*

Fields of Arbol: The Environmental Vision of C. S. Lewis (2009). His most recent book is *The Mind and the Machine: What It Means to Be Human and Why It Matters* (2011). Dickerson is a professor at Middlebury College in Vermont and the director of the New England Young Writers Conference at Breadloaf.

B. L. Gentry's poetry has appeared in the *Cortland Review, The Other Journal*, and is forthcoming in *Rhino*. Gentry is an MFA student in the Warren Wilson College Program for Writers. She lives in Oklahoma.

David Grumett is the author, with Rachel Muers, of *Theology on the Menu: Asceticism, Meat, and Christian Diet* (2010). He is a research fellow in theology at the University of Exeter and teaches theology at the University of Cambridge. His website is www.davidgrumett.com.

Ryan Harper is a graduate student in the department of religion at Princeton University, where he is completing a dissertation on contemporary southern gospel music. His poetry, essays, and articles have appeared or are forthcoming in *Litchfield Review, Ruminate, Potomac Review, Sugar House Review, Journal of Religion and Popular Culture, Huffington Post*, and elsewhere. Harper lives in New Jersey with his spouse, the writer and chaplain Lynn Casteel Harper. He is a jazz drummer, avid runner, and lover of the outdoors.

John Leax is Professor Emeritus of Houghton College in New York. His work has been widely published in periodicals and anthologies for over forty years. His volumes of poetry include *Reaching into Silence* (1974), *The Task of Adam* (1985), *Country Labors* (1991), and *Tabloid News* (2005). His works of nonfiction include *In Season and Out* (1985), *Standing Ground* (1991), and *Out Walking* (2000). *Grace Is Where I Live* (1993) was reissued in a revised and expanded edition by WordFarm in 2004, and his new collection, *Recluse Freedom: Poems 1990–2010*, is due in 2012.

Katherine Lo has an MA in English literature from Cal State Fullerton. She teaches high school English in Southern California, and she enjoys long walks and ice cream.

Robert Hill Long is the author of five books, most recently *The Kilim Dreaming* (2010), a collection of three long narrative sequences and one elegiac sequence. He lives in western Oregon.

Lee Price first developed a reverence for painting from her mother, a high school art teacher. She received her BFA from Philadelphia's Moore College of Art, later studied at the Art Student's League and the New York Academy of Art, and then studied independently with Alyssa Monks who Price cites as her greatest influence. Price's paintings have been the subject of numerous solo and group shows across the United States. She is represented by Evoke Contemporary in Sante Fe, New Mexico, and Wendt Gallery, which has showrooms in Laguna Beach, New York, Singapore, and Vienna. Lee currently lives and works in Beacon, New York.

Chelle Stearns has a PhD from the University of St. Andrews. As a practicing violinist (and lover of literature), she enjoys teaching and writing about the intersection of the Christian imagination and theology. Stearns currently teaches systematic theology at the Seattle School of Theology and Psychology.

Heather Smith Stringer is Art Editor for *The Other Journal*.

Jon Tschanz is a recent graduate of Duke Divinity School, Team Pastor at Warren W. Willis UMC Camp in Fruitland Park, Florida, and Associate Director of Branches, a division of South Florida Urban Ministries, in Florida City, Florida.

Stephen H. Webb is Professor of Religion and Philosophy at Wabash College, Crawfordsville, Indiana. He and his wife, Diane Timmerman, who is Professor of Theatre at Butler University, have four children and two dogs. Webb is the author of eleven books, including two about food: *Good Eating* (2001) and *On God and Dogs* (1998). His wife does most of the cooking.

Alissa Wilkinson teaches at the King's College in New York City and edits *Comment*. She and her husband, Tom, like the brunch at Dizzy's in Brooklyn best.

David Williams is an associate professor of philosophy at Azusa Pacific University. He lives just outside of Yosemite National Park, teaching full-time at Azusa Pacific's High Sierra Semester, a great books program integrating the humanities and outdoor education.

Norman Wirzba is Research Professor of Theology, Ecology, and Rural Life at Duke Divinity School. He pursues research and teaching interests at the intersections of theology, philosophy, ecology, and agrarian and environmental studies. Wirzba has published *The Paradise of God: Renewing Religion in an Ecological Age* (2003) and *Living the Sabbath: Discovering the Rhythms of Rest and Delight* (2006). His newest book, *Food and Faith: A Theology of Eating* (2011), is available now.